To:

_____

From:

_____

Date:

_____

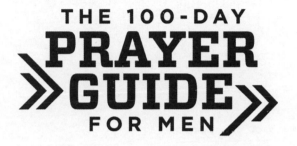

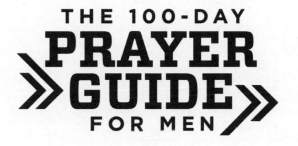

THE 100-DAY
PRAYER GUIDE
FOR MEN

GLENN
HASCALL

BARBOUR
PUBLISHING

ISBN 978-1-63609-513-4

Cover Design: Greg Jackson, Thinkpen Design

Published by Barbour Publishing, Inc., 1810 Barbour Drive, Uhrichsville, Ohio 44683, www.barbourbooks.com

Our mission is to inspire the world with the life-changing message of the Bible.

Member of the
Evangelical Christian
Publishers Association

Printed in China.

Get on the Road to a More Powerful Prayer Life

The 100-Day Prayer Guide for Men offers relatable, real-life wisdom and inspiration for prayer. You'll encounter page after page of biblical truths you can apply to your own quiet time with God.

It covers overarching topics like Praise, Confession, and Intercession, as well as more specific issues such as:

- Family
- Culture
- the Lost
- Healing
- Physical Needs
- and much more

This book provides a biblical example or teaching on each subject, a brief devotional thought, guidance on incorporating the topic into your own prayer life, and a short prayer starter.

It's a perfect way to spend your next hundred days!

1. Prayer Is Essential

Look to the LORD and his strength;
seek his face always.
1 CHRONICLES 16:11 NIV

No prayer guide would be complete without acknowledging King David, so let's start there. In spite of his many personal faults, flaws, and shortcomings, David knew prayer was essential. He conversed with God often and with passion, and many of us can quote at least one of these prayers from memory.

We will cross paths with David several times over the next hundred days. But as we begin this journey, let's simply consider his advice in 1 Chronicles 16:11. After becoming king of all Israel and bringing God's ark of the covenant to his new capital of Jerusalem, David delivered a new psalm for Asaph and his fellow temple musicians to sing before the people—and before God. One vital theme of the song is prayer—seeking the Lord and His strength, seeking His face and His presence, seeking. . .and then finding.

Notice that *seek* is an active verb. Pursuing God is up to you. You can do it through prayer, an element of life as essential as air, water, food, friendship, forgiveness, and love.

Pray because there's hope at the end of your amen, there's love in the way God responds, and there's clarity in asking God for help.

THINK ABOUT IT

- On a scale of 1 to 10, how essential has prayer been to your life lately? Why?

- What do you enjoy most about prayer? What is most difficult?

- What might need to change in your life to make room for better prayer?

PRAY ABOUT IT

- Ask God to impress the importance of prayer on your spirit.

- Request energy and focus for your time of prayer.

- Thank God for being ready and eager to hear your prayer.

Lord, I'm seeking Your face and presence.
May I find peace and power with You.

2. Call-and-Response

Then I called on the name of the LORD:
"Please, LORD, save me!" How kind
the LORD is! How good he is!
PSALM 116:4–5 NLT

The term *call-and-response* describes moments when one statement is quickly followed by an answer. Imagine, for example, two close friends who know each other so well that they finish each other's sentences. That's what prayer is.

You call and God answers. *But wait,* you might think, *I don't hear anything!* You don't have to—God's response is usually found in the Bible. Do you look there after you make your call? His response was waiting even before you called.

Other times, His Word and His instructions will call to you and ask for your response. The Bible calls everyone, for instance, to love others and obey God. How are you responding? Are you ignoring this call? Call-and-response goes both directions, and it's unfair to think God should answer your requests if you've been putting off His.

This makes prayer a vital part of your connection with God. You can share what you need, and He can share what He needs. So when He calls, respond.

He's been responding to you your whole life.

» THINK ABOUT IT

- Why is it unreasonable to think God should respond when you don't respond to Him?

- What might prevent you from answering His call?

- How can prayer be a key part of your response to God?

» PRAY ABOUT IT

- Read a Bible passage and decide how you can take what you learn and respond to God.

- Write down thoughts that help you respond.

- Call out to God in prayer and then spend time in His Word to discover His response.

Your call is important to me, God.
Help me respond like You do.

3. Don't Break the Connection

Do not be anxious about anything, but in every situation, by prayer and petition, with thanksgiving, present your requests to God.
PHILIPPIANS 4:6 NIV

Anxiety wears you out. It drags you down. It makes it hard to breathe. But guess what? You can stop it!

Philippians 4:6 is a good example of a call-and-response prayer. You call, and God responds, "Tell Me what you need—and bring gratitude." But how can you be grateful for life's drudgeries and fears? By showing gratitude in response to God's call, you're thanking Him for the future outcome, not just for the present struggle that caused you to make the call.

Prayer should always be a back-and-forth response. You call, and God responds—He calls, and you *need* to respond. Today's verse clearly says that your prayer is a perfect response to His call. Praying proves you were paying attention—and it means He's paying attention to you.

When you call, don't doubt God's response or just view it as good information that might come in handy later. Both choices break the call-and-response connection between your heart and God's.

» THINK ABOUT IT

- Do you sometimes find it easier to consider God's call optional?

- Do you often think your call requires an immediate response?

- How can you demonstrate that you are serious about God's call—and your response?

» PRAY ABOUT IT

- Create a list of your worries and share them with God.

- Use today's prayer as an opportunity to respond to His call.

- Express gratitude for God's love and His willingness to help you.

Father, may worry never be my go-to response.
Help me call and learn from Your response.

4. No Street Performance

*When thou prayest, enter into thy closet, and
when thou hast shut thy door, pray to thy
Father which is in secret; and thy Father which
seeth in secret shall reward thee openly.*
MATTHEW 6:6 KJV

Street performers live to impress others. They accept a cobblestone path, park bench, or curb as a stage. Their performances tell inspiring stories, and their audiences often applaud and toss in a loose bill or spare change to show their appreciation.

This platform may work well to advertise your performance skills, but it's a horrible platform for personal prayer. God doesn't view His conversation with you as a new off-Broadway play. There's a time and place for group prayer, but God wants your personal prayer to come from your heart, not from a desire to be noticed.

Your prayer to God isn't meant to impress the masses. God has never wanted you to turn your unique and special conversation with Him into a street performance. The Bible describes people who did that, and God was neither amused nor impressed. Personal prayer and personal response, however, combine in a way that pleases God and keeps you focused.

» THINK ABOUT IT

- What is your response when you see people who pray to be noticed?

- How does that kind of prayer differ from a call-and-response prayer?

- Why do you think people choose to pray arrogant prayers?

» PRAY ABOUT IT

- Pray as if God is the only one who's listening, even if you're in public.

- When you pray, leave ego at the door.

- Effective prayers don't have to be polished, so keep praying.

I have burdens, Lord. Help me share them honestly with You and refuse to worry about what others think.

5. Every Day— Every Situation

Pray continually.
1 THESSALONIANS 5:17 NIV

To say that prayer isn't essential would be like saying food or oxygen aren't that important. To say that prayer is something you only bring out as a last resort is like saying love is a nice, if unnecessary, add-on to your life. Honesty prevents you from going that far. Prayer has always been essential.

Prayer is not just a tool that's only useful in a specific circumstance—it's vital every day and in every situation.

"Just how important to God," you may ask, "is prayer?" Well, just know that the Bible mentions prayer more times than there are days in the year—and it describes prayer even more. God wants prayer to be a critical component of your relationship with Him. Life without prayer is like having a friend you never talk to—it's nonsensical.

Good days or bad days? It doesn't matter—pray. Prayer will always be the connection between your need and God's answer. It invites you to leave your three-ring circus and stand in the throne room of God.

Doesn't that sound better than worry?

» THINK ABOUT IT

- Why is it important that you see prayer as a first response?

- Is anything preventing you from diving into prayer consistently?

- How does knowing that God wants you to come to Him change your attitude toward prayer?

» PRAY ABOUT IT

- Admit God wants you to pray as often as possible.

- Find ways to remind yourself to pray.

- When you wonder if it's a good time to pray—pray.

---

*I don't bother You, God. May every
moment of my life convince me to pray.*

6. Prayers You Were Trying to Pray

The Holy Spirit helps us in our weakness.
For example, we don't know what God wants us
to pray for. But the Holy Spirit prays for us with
groanings that cannot be expressed in words.

ROMANS 8:26 NLT

There are three scenarios in which you might be tempted not to pray: (1) you blew it and are tempted to hide from God; (2) your world seems to be falling apart, and putting your feelings into words is impossible; (3) you're overwhelmingly amazed by God's goodness, and your mind is moving faster than your mouth. In each of these situations, you might say, "Dear God," and then go silent, because nothing else will make the trip to your tongue.

God's Spirit lives with you, so He knows you. When words fail you, they won't fail God's Spirit. He can pick up where you left off, praying for you in a way that understands your need.

You can pray even when you don't know if you're doing it right. You can pray when you're learning. You can pray when words seem inadequate.

When you are overwhelmed, God can still listen to your heart, know your mind, and answer the prayer you were trying to pray.

 THINK ABOUT IT

- Do you find some prayers difficult to pray? Why?

- How can knowing that God's Spirit can pray for you give you the courage to start praying?

- Why is not knowing what to pray never a good reason to stop?

» PRAY ABOUT IT

- Ask God to remind you that you are not alone when you pray.

- Pray what you can—God even understands silence.

- Thank God for the help His Spirit provides.

When my words won't show up, Father,
I'm thankful that Your Spirit will.

7. Get Connected— Pay Attention

[God said,] "Call to me and I will answer you and tell you great and unsearchable things you do not know."
JEREMIAH 33:3 NIV

Have you ever known someone—maybe a grandpa, neighbor, teacher, or dad—who seemed to offer new wisdom with every conversation? That person probably told vivid stories that illustrated what you should avoid in life and what you should do. This is the most effective form of sharing advice, as it sticks in your mind and forces you to consider other perspectives.

Prayer does the same thing for the Christian life. It's quality time with the greatest author in the universe. He knows everything, and He can teach truth in two ways: the stories found in His Word and our own personal adventures.

You'll notice God doesn't say He shares this conversation with everyone. No, He said you should "call to Him" first. Come to Him like a boy eagerly asking his dad to tell him a story—you'll receive a lifetime of bedtime blessings, early morning encounters, and midday memories.

God is ready to share His response. So call, get connected, and pay attention.

» THINK ABOUT IT

- Do you sometimes hesitate to ask God for help understanding His plan?

- How does it help to consider the Christian life as a great adventure with God?

- Why is it important to remember God is the author of your story?

» PRAY ABOUT IT

- Pray for God to give you the wisdom to understand.

- Ask for the stories that will inspire.

- Tell God you are willing to go on this adventure with Him.

I always learn when I spend time with You, Lord.
Give me a fresh opportunity to learn today.

8. Prayer Is Your Big Job

*Praying always with all prayer and supplication
in the Spirit, and watching thereunto with all
perseverance and supplication for all saints.*
EPHESIANS 6:18 KJV

Supplication is the act of begging for something earnestly or humbly. You could just replace it with the word *ask*, but that would leave out the attitudes that come with it.

The word *supplication* is used twice in Ephesians 6:18. Also, to add to the idea of prayer's intensity, the word *perseverance* is included. If this sounds like prayer is a spiritual workout, that's because it is!

This verse urges us to never give up, even when we think God is too busy or uninterested. Many years ago, people referred to this kind of prayer as "praying through." Persevering prayer never says, "Well I asked, and didn't get it. I'm out." No, it holds on, hopes long, and believes God can do anything.

So pray, supplicate, and persevere for the entire family of God. It may be a big job, but it's yours.

≫ THINK ABOUT IT

- How has the word *supplicate* enhanced your thoughts about prayer?

- What is it about supplication that can help you see prayer as an adventure?

- Are your prayers more than a memorized bedtime blessing?

≫ PRAY ABOUT IT

- Think of the Christians you know best and pray for them as specifically as possible.

- When prayer seems hard, determine to stick with it.

- Ask God for help remembering other Christians so that it seems natural to pray for them.

You want me to pray and never give up, God. Let me supplicate earnestly, persistently, and humbly.

9. More Than a Judge's Score

*[Jesus said,] "When you pray, do not be
like the hypocrites, for they love to pray
standing in the synagogues and on the street
corners to be seen by others. Truly I tell you,
they have received their reward in full."*

MATTHEW 6:5 NIV

These are the praying men Jesus warned you about. They
were two-faced hypocrites, praying only to be seen. They
were actors, just like the people you read about five days
ago. But between then and now, you've had the chance to
see prayer as an authentic, persistent adventure designed
for people who've failed.

Prayer is so much greater than a judge's score. It's a sacred
honor to talk to the God who made you, and He places
absolutely no restrictions on when and how often you can
get in touch.

Yet God knows that if you set aside real, meaningful prayer
for shallow words, you waste your time. Jesus said your
prayers should express humility—any touch of pride will be
seen (and mocked) by the observant.

Make sure your prayers point your audience to God and
make them interested in learning more.

» THINK ABOUT IT

- Why can prayer hypocrites be thought of as two-faced?

- What is it about inauthentic prayer that displeases God?

- How can you guard your prayers from becoming a performance?

» PRAY ABOUT IT

- Ask God for the wisdom to seek His attention more than anyone else's.

- Prayer is a conversation, so what you pray should sound like a discussion with a friend.

- Dedicate your prayer time to being real with God.

I want to be open and honest with You, Father. Help me be bold and humble in coming to You to talk.

10. Outsider No More

"If my people who are called by my name
will humble themselves and pray and seek
my face and turn from their wicked ways,
I will hear from heaven and will forgive
their sins and restore their land."
2 Chronicles 7:14 NLT

When it comes to God, who do you think you are? An outsider? Troublemaker? Lawbreaker? What about forgiven? Loved? Rescued?

Sometimes, it's possible to find yourself somewhere in-between. Maybe you're loved, forgiven, and rescued all the time, but you're also an outsider, troublemaker, and lawbreaker on occasion. If so, God wants you to give up this part-time gig. He wants you to remember the new name of "Christian" that you wear.

You're encouraged to remember that God is God. . .and that you still sin. Don't show up before God stiff-arming His forgiveness by refusing to admit your mistakes. He wants you to turn your back on that life.

If you do this when you pray, God is all ears. He pays attention when you humbly request forgiveness—and He no longer sees you as an outsider.

» THINK ABOUT IT

- Why is it possible to be accepted by God and still feel like an outsider?

- How can you refuse the title of troublemaker and lawbreaker forever?

- What is most important in your regular conversations with God?

» PRAY ABOUT IT

- Ask God to teach you how He truly sees you.

- Remember that God doesn't owe you something— He's given you everything.

- Spend time telling God what you know about yourself.

I would love to be remembered as forgiven, loved, and rescued, Lord. Take this troublemaker and change his status.

11. No Restrictions— No Exclusions

I will therefore that men pray every where.
1 Timothy 2:8 KJV

When the power grid is compromised, public utilities might place a "rolling brown out" into effect. During a brown out, a portion of the population has no power for an hour or so, and then their power is turned on while another section is turned off. This method allows the power to stay on for the majority of people whenever there's not enough for everyone.

God has no prayer brown outs. He's never overwhelmed, so He doesn't cut off the communication you have with Him. Instead, the Bible suggests that you should pray in *all* locations. Even in a place where everyone else is breaking the law? Yes. Even when you're all alone? Yes. Even if it's the dead of night? Yes.

When you call, God will respond. When you ask, He will answer. When your need is genuine, He is arranging delivery. Prayer doesn't depend on a geographic location, a scheduled time, or even your skill in praying.

There are no restrictions, no exclusions, and no waiting.

» THINK ABOUT IT

- What might cause someone to want to avoid praying?

- Have you ever thought that now is a bad time to pray?

- Why is it helpful knowing there is no wrong place or time to pray?

» PRAY ABOUT IT

- Ask God for reassurance that you can pray whenever you need to.

- Believe that you can talk to God wherever you are.

- Thank God for listening all day long—every day.

You don't make me wait, God. I can pray everywhere, and that makes all the difference.

12. Prayers a Wise God Answers

This is the confidence we have in approaching God: that if we ask anything according to his will, he hears us.

1 JOHN 5:14 NIV

Does God have to comply with everything you ask? First John 5:14 might sound that way at first glance. But think about it: such a scenario would mean God isn't in control—you are. Does that sound like something a wise God would allow?

God isn't offering a blank check approach to prayer. Instead, there's a subtle but all-important disclaimer in this verse— "according to His will."

If you ask for something He already wants you to have, then it's an easy yes (although sometimes, you might not get it right away). If you're asking for something His Word forbids, then no matter how often you ask for it, that request will always be denied. God will not give you anything that would be harmful or would stop His plan for your life. You might be able to get some of these things on your own, but they'll never be God's gift.

» THINK ABOUT IT

- Why is it incorrect to think God says yes to every request?

- Why is it wiser to let God decide what He gives?

- How can you learn to be comfortable with God's decisions?

» PRAY ABOUT IT

- Ask God to help you learn what He does and doesn't want for you.

- Once you learn what God wants, find ways He can use you to get them done.

- Offer God your willingness to obey His rules.

Forgive me for thinking You have to say yes to my prayers, Father. Instead, help me say yes to following Your plan.

13. No Great Distance

Before daybreak the next morning, Jesus got up and went out to an isolated place to pray.
MARK 1:35 NLT

People will go to extraordinary lengths—sometimes traveling hundreds of miles—to talk with someone they love.

When you want to talk to God, you don't have to travel. You can talk to Him right here and right now. But first, you must *want* to talk to Him. He's not an inconvenience, obligation, or item on your spiritual to-do list. He's already involved in every aspect of your life, so He wants you to be involved in His.

Examples are important, and Jesus is the most important of them all. He was bold in coming to God, wise in making time to visit, and courageous enough to prioritize it over sleep. He didn't miss an opportunity to get in touch and experience God's presence. While everyone slept, Jesus got up and found a quiet place. Prayer was that important.

Today, God is talking to you through the Bible. Are you talking to Him through prayer?

 THINK ABOUT IT

- What can you do to make prayer a priority?

- Why is prayer more than just one more item on a crowded checklist?

- How do you become more intentional about including prayer as an everyday opportunity?

» PRAY ABOUT IT

- Ask God to give you a fresh perspective on the value of prayer.

- Invite God to show you what you need to know in the Bible.

- Determine that you will pray today and then listen for God's response.

There are things I can only say to You, Lord. Help me take the time to speak the words I need to share with You.

14. Use Prayer to Praise

Let us continually offer to God a
sacrifice of praise—the fruit of lips
that openly profess his name.
HEBREWS 13:15 NIV

God's Word is so rich that sometimes we just have to slow down and take a deep look at what's being said. Hebrews 13:15 is a great example.

Let us—this verse is for you and everyone you know.

Continually—perpetually, always, and never-ending.

Offer to God—give Him a gift that He wants and that you can give.

A sacrifice of praise—being intentional about honoring God, even when you don't feel like it, is important.

The fruit of lips—the words you use will grow in your heart and shine through in your prayer. Grow a good crop.

That openly profess His name—it would be wrong to be ashamed of your good God. Use His name honorably and remember the amazing things He's done.

Praise starts in the heart before it reaches your mouth. It is the understanding that you're not alone. . .and that the one who is with you is better than anyone else. His answers are perfect, His love unrivaled, and His plans unequaled.

Remember what He's done so that you can be confident in what He'll do. Use your prayers to praise.

THINK ABOUT IT

- Does praise ever seem like the hardest part of prayer?

- What praiseworthy thing is God doing in your life?

- How can you use today's verse as a roadmap for praise?

 ## PRAY ABOUT IT

- Think of three things you're thankful for and use each one as a reason for praise.

- Ask God to help you remember His goodness.

- Take note of life events and use these memories to inspire praise toward God.

I want my lips to display a good memory,
God. Help me remember and then tell You
what Your goodness means to me.

15. The Joy Journey

*Shout with joy to the LORD, all the
earth! Worship the LORD with gladness.
Come before him, singing with joy.*
PSALM 100:1–2 NLT

Many scholars believe Moses might've written Psalm 100. If so, the event that inspired this psalm could have been the Exodus from Egypt or the rescue through the Red Sea. Whatever its motivation, the song describes an epic God in epic terms, giving reasons to praise Him.

Frankly, the backstory behind the psalm may be less important than the praise that gushes from the page in brilliant color. This isn't a quiet moment of worship—it's a full-on, crowd-shouting explosion of joy. The invitation was sent and no one was left out, even those who turned their backs, closed their doors, and plugged their ears.

This is a joy that a man experiences when his soldier son or daughter comes safely home, when he sees his prodigal son in the distance, or when his bride comes walking down the aisle. It is pure joy—cherished and unleashed. Each of us was made to experience this celebration.

Over the next few days, join this praise parade and make Psalm 100 a vital part of your prayer life.

THINK ABOUT IT

- Does the idea of "epic" praise excite or intimidate you? Why?

- What does the exclamation mark in today's passage mean to you?

- When was the last time you experienced joy in times of prayer?

PRAY ABOUT IT

- Ask God to help you develop joy in your prayer journey.

- Seek reasons to praise God.

- Write down moments that brought you joy, and then tell God all about them.

When joy doesn't describe my prayer life,
Father, remind me of Your goodness.

16. You're God's Amazing Design

Acknowledge that the LORD is God! He made us, and we are his. We are his people, the sheep of his pasture.
PSALM 100:3 NLT

Sometimes, the best way to bring joy to your prayer life is to bring your acknowledgement of God's goodness. This isn't the old, tired meal blessing, "God is great, God is good, let us thank Him for our food." Rather, this is a more personal appraisal of what God has actually done: What events can't be explained without invoking God's blessing or providence?

Think about your body, for instance, and declare that it's God's creation. This amazing design does things that can't be explained without God. There would need to be far too many coincidences for it to happen naturally.

God made you—you are His. When you know Him, you join His flock of sheep. Sheep follow their shepherd, and they are best when they stick together.

Today, you must decide: Will you acknowledge that God is good, or will you set the acknowledgement aside and just tell God what you need? He welcomes both, but He also knows that your acknowledgement does much more to change you.

» THINK ABOUT IT

- Has acknowledging God ever impacted your life?
- How will acknowledging God change your prayer experience?
- What can make acknowledging God difficult?

» PRAY ABOUT IT

- Thank God for acknowledging you.
- Ask for insight to further understand God's goodness.
- Identify ways to acknowledge God—and then acknowledge Him!

Lord, You are more than the place where I go to provide general customer feedback. Help me acknowledge the ways that You amaze me each day.

17. A Time to Show Up

*Enter his gates with thanksgiving; go
into his courts with praise. Give thanks
to him and praise his name.*
PSALM 100:4 NLT

If you're keeping track, then you'll remember that you arrive in prayer with joy and then acknowledge God's goodness. . .but that's not the end. Gratitude—which flows from the awareness of God's help—arrives next.

With every step in this process, you move from your world to His. And as you pass the gates into His court, everything you learn leads you to a place of personal praise. Ultimately, God even welcomes you into His throne room.

When you don't express thanks, however, it may be because you're taking God for granted by internally crediting either yourself or mere chance for your blessings. Just know that when you do this, you are left at the gate. There, you'll be stuck passing notes somewhere outside His kingdom instead of talking with Him face-to-face.

When God invites you inside His throne room for a visit, never be too stubborn to accept!

THINK ABOUT IT

- Is meeting God with gratitude sometimes too overwhelming to you? Why?

- Why should you add thanks and praise to your prayers?

- Why are some people too stubborn to praise God?

 PRAY ABOUT IT

- Before you pray again, think of three things you're thankful for.

- Determine one way you will add praise to your next prayer.

- In moments when you're not praying, remember your amazing God.

You gave me life, and I'm grateful, God.
You gave me love, and I praise You.

18. Fellowship of the Forgiven

For the LORD is good. His unfailing love
continues forever, and his faithfulness
continues to each generation.
PSALM 100:5 NLT

You are not the first to be invited to speak with God, and you won't be the last. But instead of decreasing prayer's value, this news should give you a greater sense of awe: God hasn't grown tired of His human creation.

He could've put up an OUT FOR LUNCH sign or refused your call due to lack of interest, but He didn't. Instead, God continues to enjoy conversation with you because you still mean the world to Him. The next step is yours to take, but you're never forced to take it. The change is yours to embrace, and God can help you make it. The outcome is yours to accept, and God hopes you will.

Prayer is an epic new adventure every day. You are in tune with a good God who expresses an unfailing love and undying faithfulness toward you and everyone else.

So today, reconsider your adventure in praise. Discover joy, acknowledge God's goodness, express gratitude, and make praise a standard response. God has always been faithful, and He's offering a fantastic journey with the fellowship of the forgiven.

» THINK ABOUT IT

- Does the idea of God's faithfulness comfort you when you pray?

- How can you experience a greater awe of God?

- How can you praise God for His forgiveness?

» PRAY ABOUT IT

- Thank God for His faithfulness.

- Thank God for His forgiveness.

- Thank God for the goodness that invites conversation.

---

*You're faithful and I'm forgiven, Father.
I accept Your invitation to pray, and I'm
bringing thanks and praise with me.*

19. Praise Past the Prayer

*Let my mouth be filled with thy praise
and with thy honour all the day.*

PSALM 71:8 KJV

When praise is added to your prayer life, it won't likely stop between your "Dear God" and your "Amen." Once you recognize how good God is, it'll spill out in every conversation you have with others. Why? Because the more someone means to you, the more you'll talk about them. An example: if you're a new grandparent, then you'll give coworkers and friends regular status updates about every new thing that your grandchild does.

Translate this kind of enthusiasm to your friendship with God. Imagine being as excited about God as you are about your son's baseball stats or your daughter's science fair presentation. Everyone agrees that you have every right to be thrilled with your kids, spouse, or grandkids, so why would you ever hide the amazingness of God?

Never let your praise and honor stop once your time of prayer has ended—after all, God's blessings don't! His goodness rolls on to everyone, even to those who have never prayed.

THINK ABOUT IT

- Are you frightened or excited by the idea of taking praise beyond your prayers?

- What stories of God's goodness will you share with others?

- Why is it important to honor God publicly?

PRAY ABOUT IT

- Pay attention to the impact of praise in your prayers, and then share the highlights with others.

- Ask God to show you ways to make Him a priority in conversation.

- Spend time studying what the Bible says about praise.

People need to know that You're amazing, Lord.
Help me speak words that honor You best.

20. Past's Positive Impact

*LORD, you are my God; I will exalt you and praise
your name, for in perfect faithfulness you have
done wonderful things, things planned long ago.*
ISAIAH 25:1 NIV

God doesn't make impulse decisions. His plan for this world
isn't new, and His master plan needs no revisions, addendums,
or annexes. Nothing takes Him by surprise.

Humanity plans their own quests, but God's plans existed
long before your grandparent's grandparents were born.
When it comes to praise, don't just stop with *your* history—
look at the history of humanity itself. There, you'll find God's
fingerprints, leaving you with no choice other than to praise
Him for His incredible deeds.

The command to praise came long before any nation
or set of human laws was established. And the things God
planned long ago are still having a positive impact on your
present and future.

Keep learning more, and you'll have all the reason in the
world to praise Him!

» THINK ABOUT IT

- How does knowing God's plans are not new help you appreciate Him more?

- Why is the old command to praise still as relevant as it was at first?

- What can this history teach you about God?

» PRAY ABOUT IT

- Thank God for showing His goodness throughout history.

- Consider God's promises and understand that He continues to keep them.

- Ask God for a greater appreciation for His goodness.

History teaches me that You are perfectly faithful, God. Thanks for making and keeping promises for my good and for Your glory.

21. When Life Gets Loud

[Sing] psalms and hymns and spiritual
songs among yourselves, and [make]
music to the Lord in your hearts.
Ephesians 5:19 nlt

Prayer can be something you do even when you don't have your hands folded and your eyes closed. It's a communion with the God who supplies everything you need. This kind of prayer happens when you read psalms about God and sing songs that teach you more about His character. These are all part of the conversation you should be having with God.

There's a rhythm and dynamic range to God's love, grace, and mercy. It's the soundtrack of reality and a continuation of prayer.

You can worship in your home, car, or business. You may get on your knees to pray, but the conversation can continue when you're swinging a hammer, helping customers, or calming your child in a thunderstorm. Prayer can be a very private, solitary conversation with God, but you should also make God your companion everywhere you go.

You don't have to leave Him behind when life gets loud. In fact, that may be when you need Him the most.

» THINK ABOUT IT

- Do you ever treat prayer as a portable experience?
- Why should you never leave God behind?
- How can you use some of the ideas in Ephesians 5:19 to take God with you today?

» PRAY ABOUT IT

- Express praise by reading a psalm to God.
- Take prayer to your vocal chords and sing a hymn or worship song to God.
- No matter where you are, take the time to discuss the hard things with God.

From reading Your Word, I know You're interested in music, Father. Help me use music as a part of prayer that encourages both of us.

22. With Every Breath

Let every thing that hath breath praise
the LORD. Praise ye the LORD.
PSALM 150:6 KJV

Who should be offering praise to God? Some people? Most people? No. If you breathe, you should be marveling at God's wonder. He created the Grand Canyon and yet knows your name. He created the oceans—and all the fish they contain—and He wants to talk with you. He created the intricate design of the eye and asks you to look for Him.

Those who will not praise are misinformed. Everything God made is designed to allow every living creature to make the same beautiful conclusion: God made this, and there's no one like Him. Even when you didn't know Him, you had all the evidence you needed to know that someone bigger than any human was behind all of this.

Because you breathe—praise God. Because you've been given a mind to understand—praise God. Because you've discovered the Creator and found that there's none besides Him—praise God.

» THINK ABOUT IT

- Could you possibly think of a reason to refuse to praise God?

- How does creation itself convince you praise is essential?

- Why do you think some people try their best to deny God exists?

» PRAY ABOUT IT

- Explore nature or view some nature photos online and tell God what you see.

- Ask God to help you understand the value of praise when you see His beauty.

- Connect God's creation with His love for you and tell Him why this matters.

Make praise an everyday part of prayer for me, Lord. Help me remember that You created impossible beauty so that I could recognize You and say, "Thanks!"

23. His Strong Arm

The strong right arm of the LORD has done glorious things! . . . I will live to tell what the LORD has done.
Psalm 118:16–17 NLT

You are encountering another moment with King David. The king faced personal and professional battles, and things hadn't always gone his way. Yet the king saw God's goodness every day and, in this prelude to prayer, boldly praises Him for the glorious things He has done.

That's exactly what you're called to do. When you pray, use whatever you're learning about God to praise Him. When you're facing the unknown, spend time reviewing the known. If God has always been good, stop doubting His continued goodness. Because God is loving, accept His love.

You don't always need to come to God empty and broken. Don't misunderstand; brokenness is one of the primary reasons to come to God in prayer. But don't miss the opportunity to marvel at answered prayer, unexpected protection, and impossible miracles.

Because God has come to your rescue, let other people know all about it!

» THINK ABOUT IT

- What kind of encouragement can you be to others who face struggles that God has helped you with?

- Why is it important to piece together the story of God's goodness in your life?

- How can acknowledging God's role in your life improve your prayer experience?

» PRAY ABOUT IT

- Ask God for wisdom to see His work in your life.

- Review God's goodness and then tell Him what you learned.

- Follow God's instructions when life seems the most difficult.

I don't always see what You've done for me, God. Give me the insight to recognize Your work and praise You for it.

24. The Kneeling

O come, let us worship and bow down:
let us kneel before the LORD our maker.
PSALM 95:6 KJV

In the story of King Arthur and the Knights of the Round Table, all the warriors had a specific way of honoring their king: they placed the tip of their sword in the ground, put their hands on the hilt, bent one knee, and bowed their head. This action proclaimed their loyalty to the king alone.

It should come as no surprise that David, an earthly king, encouraged people who paid honor to him to also join him in honoring God. The visual is powerful—a crowned king kneels with his head bowed before the God who gave him his strength and power. This humbling act let everyone know there is one greater, wiser, stronger, and more honorable than the king.

The king could've told his people to follow his example, but he instead admitted he was unworthy to lead the people. He honored another and asked everyone to do the same. Pride had no place at this remarkable moment in time.

THINK ABOUT IT

- What makes the picture of kneeling so important?

- Why is honoring God a valuable part of praise?

- How can you determine to dethrone pride and honor God?

》 PRAY ABOUT IT

- Imagine yourself kneeling before God and tell Him why He is worthy.

- Ask God to help you see the value in humble worship.

- Try describing the joy you feel in serving alongside the greatest King of all.

---

*Even when I can't kneel with my body, Father,
I'll kneel with my heart. You are worthy
of my worship, and I will follow You.*

25. As Long as You Live

*I will praise the LORD all my life; I will sing
praise to my God as long as I live.*
PSALM 146:2 NIV

How long is too long to praise God? You could spend every minute of every day of every year, and it *still* wouldn't touch the praise that God deserves. You can't overdo praise (just ask King David!) but it's an amazing blessing to try.

There's no end to the things you could praise God for. Sometimes, it's easier to overlook some of the smaller things, but life's richness would fade if they were to disappear. Each gift that God supplies has a purpose and impacts your life.

It isn't worthless to thank God for the little things. God is big, and He takes care of everything large and small. He knows the number of hairs on your head and even pays attention when a lone sparrow falls from the sky.

Like a symphony with many instruments and complementary notes, even the tiniest things combine to form something mighty in God's hands. Every day, you can praise Him for His most beautiful song.

» THINK ABOUT IT

- Why is it so easy to overlook some of God's greatest work?

- What can you do to pay more attention to what God is doing?

- How is it possible to make praise a part of every prayer?

» PRAY ABOUT IT

- Ask God to allow you to see the small things that you usually overlook.

- Follow God's roadmap of miracles and celebrate each one.

- Speak words of worship when you make the choice to pray.

Help me see the many miracles I have missed, Lord. There is more to Your amazing life than I have noticed.

26. After Sorrow, Joy

You have turned my mourning into joyful dancing. You have taken away my clothes of mourning and clothed me with joy.

PSALM 30:11 NLT

Sorrow is a consequence of living. You don't want it, and you certainly don't choose it, yet it still shows up. Sadness can be followed by depression, which then produces hot angry tears at life's seeming unfairness. But somehow, God allows it.

But here's the good news: God then sends joy, promising that if you accept it, He'll take your sorrow. This joy is far deeper than mere happiness—it's a solid certainty that no matter what sorrow comes, God has an impressive outcome. It's knowing that God can be trusted with the result. It's recognizing that He is good. It's trading your rags for a new, shiny wardrobe.

This too is part of praise. It's the process of using sorrow's pain to examine God's goodness until you see that sorrow might simply be the promise of a greater joy.

When you are sorrowful, just remember that this isn't the end: more of God's story is on the way.

THINK ABOUT IT

- Do you find it easier to focus on sorrow without anticipating joy?

- What might be stopping you from experiencing joy when trouble visits?

- How does it change things for you to know that joy is available to those in trouble?

 ## PRAY ABOUT IT

- Spend time talking to God about whatever makes you sad.

- Think of the things that God has done for you and tell Him what you discover.

- If you struggle to see God's goodness, spend time paying attention when you're not praying.

You know that I struggle, God.
Remind me that Your joy is on the way.

27. True Confession

*If we confess our sins, he is faithful
and just to forgive us our sins, and to
cleanse us from all unrighteousness.*

1 JOHN 1:9 KJV

Confession is hard. It's not that the words are difficult to pronounce; rather, the struggle comes from what it means to say them. Confession means admitting you are wrong and God is right. It declares that you chose not to do the right thing. Confession has no room for pride, and pride has no interest in confession. One, however, will win the day, and confession is the only choice that restores your broken relationship with God.

God made an amazing promise to you: if you'll set pride aside and admit that you've sinned, He'll forgive your sins and wipe your record clean. His faithfulness says the penalty for sin is fully paid—it's your confession that brings forgiveness to darkened hearts.

Forgiveness isn't offered to those who won't ask. A clean record isn't extended to those who won't admit they're wrong. But this isn't just about saying words you don't want to say— it's about taking ownership of your actions, turning away from bad choices, and crying to your Father, "I've blown it, God!"

That's when you are most ready to accept His help—when the inner rebel catches a glimpse at a better life with better decisions inspired by a good God.

THINK ABOUT IT

- Why does pride make confession hard?

- Besides pride, what else has made confession hard for you?

- How can what you've learned about praise impact a willingness to confess sin?

» PRAY ABOUT IT

- Ask God to help you understand His rules.

- Study confession and admit when you make wrong choices.

- Pray for wisdom to obey.

I don't always follow Your rules, Father.
Help me learn them, trust You, and
confess my broken choices.

28. Stop Pretending

*People who conceal their sins will not
prosper, but if they confess and turn
from them, they will receive mercy.*

PROVERBS 28:13 NLT

Have you ever tried lying to God? How'd that work out
for you? If you think it's possible to keep anything from
God, you need to remember that He knows everything—even
your thoughts. You can't confess a sin that He's unaware of.
Nothing will surprise Him. He was with you when you broke
His law, so trying to hide your sin is even more futile than
trying to convince yourself that you're innocent.

You can't find forgiveness or long-term success when you
won't admit you were wrong. Maybe the reason confession is
good for the soul is that it makes you stop pretending. After
all, God doesn't appreciate hypocrisy.

Breaking God's law doesn't just make you guilty—it ensures
the death penalty. But when you confess your sin by admitting you were wrong, something incredible and unexpected
happens: God forgives you, removes the penalty, and offers
mercy.

This can only happen when you stop pretending and start
confessing.

» THINK ABOUT IT

- Have you ever tried to hide a sin from God?
- What makes denying your sin a bad choice?
- When is the perfect time to confess? Why?

» PRAY ABOUT IT

- Ask for the wisdom to admit it when you sin.
- Learn more about why sin is so important to God.
- Don't hide when you can speak to God and find forgiveness.

I sin, Lord. When I do, help me admit it so that I can discover mercy and forgiveness.

29. Bold in the Declaration of Failure

Then I acknowledged my sin to you and did not cover up my iniquity. I said, "I will confess my transgressions to the LORD." And you forgave the guilt of my sin.
PSALM 32:5 NIV

Confession isn't just a New Testament concept. King David recognized that prayer involves cause and effect—confession results in forgiveness. The king acknowledged that when it came to God's laws, he blew it. But rather than choosing the varying shades of camouflage that are intended to hide the obvious, David chose the bold color of confession.

David went even further in his confession, however, by being bold in his declaration of failure. It's not that David was bragging to God about the laws he'd broken; rather, the king was bold because he *knew* that God would forgive him if he confessed. He was bold because he believed God's promise. But he was also humble, given that he regretted his choice to break God's law and was very aware of his need for confession.

When you seek forgiveness, you don't need to be timid. But you also don't need to be so filled with pride that you won't admit your mistake.

The only thing you need is God.

» THINK ABOUT IT

- How can you be both humble and bold when you confess?
- What is the value of declaring your failure?
- How would you define the bold colors of confession?

» PRAY ABOUT IT

- Ask for help in refusing sin choices today.
- Confess sin, admit failure, and accept mercy.
- Come to God confessing your sin. . .and expect forgiveness.

I am imperfect, God. I have broken Your laws, and I am broken. I am wrong—but You are forgiving.

30. What Happens When You Confess

*I said, L*ORD*, be merciful unto me: heal my soul; for I have sinned against thee.*
PSALM 41:4 KJV

Have you ever received something you didn't deserve? That's grace. Have you ever deserved something you didn't get? That's mercy. God has been known to give both—often simultaneously. Because you've sinned, the only thing you deserve is the death sentence. Yet God's mercy chooses not to pass judgment—instead, it reminds you of the value of second chances. Because you've been redeemed by Jesus' sacrifice, you also get grace, a gift you could never earn.

This is great intel when it comes to prayer. This time of communication with God is where you admit sin, which in turn invites help that you don't deserve and withholds the judgment that you do.

King David requested mercy and asked God to heal his soul. Why? He had sinned. David admitted it, knowing that sin damages spiritual life. If he didn't deal with the sin, he would struggle to thrive. So David looked to the outcome of his prayer.

There is plenty happening during prayer: blessings are given to those who confess their spiritual sickness, and mercy and healing are bestowed upon those who seek remedy.

» THINK ABOUT IT

- What is the difference between mercy and grace?
- How is confession a way to be restored?
- What is God really doing for you when He forgives?

» PRAY ABOUT IT

- Ask God for mercy when you confess your sin.
- Describe your struggle to Him and admit your guilt.
- Give God the freedom to heal you spiritually.

---

*I don't deserve mercy, but I need it, Father.
Life isn't easy, and I don't always walk
the right path. Heal what's broken inside
and help me follow more closely.*

31. Lawbreaker

*Seek the LORD while you can find him. Call
on him now while he is near. Let the wicked
change their ways and banish the very thought
of doing wrong. Let them turn to the LORD
that he may have mercy on them. Yes, turn
to our God, for he will forgive generously.*

ISAIAH 55:6–7 NLT

Criminals do everything they possibly can not to get caught. They refuse to talk to anyone about what they did. They may leave town looking for a place to hide. They might even try to compensate for their crime by doing as many good things as possible. But nothing changes the fact that they broke the law.

God can be found through prayer, but the wicked have trouble locating Him because they keep hiding. It's hard to turn toward God when you're running away from Him. Mercy and forgiveness are waiting, but the unrepentant sinner will never notice.

In a courtroom, confession happens when suspects admit they broke the law. Similarly, God wants you to know and own up to the crime you've committed. Remember: pride makes you hide from God while humility admits sin and is surprised by mercy and forgiveness.

» THINK ABOUT IT

- Why can't the wicked find God?
- What would make it easier to turn toward God?
- How can you keep from hiding from God?

» PRAY ABOUT IT

- Turn from sin so that you can recognize God.
- Express sorrow for the sins you've committed.
- Thank God when He gives you wisdom to make a better choice.

I feel badly about breaking Your laws, so move my feet in Your direction, Lord. Thank You for teaching me that I don't have to run any longer.

32. The Great Impact

Peter was kept in prison, but the church
was earnestly praying to God for him.
ACTS 12:5 NIV

When someone is going through a health crisis, job loss, or financial disaster, it's safe to say that person is overwhelmed.

If you know anyone who fits this description (or if that person is you), then your mind should move to prayer. You can pray for others, and they can pray for you. The Bible calls this "intercession," which means speaking to God on behalf of someone else.

God is aware of their need, but are you? Do you care enough about other people to mention their needs to God? This isn't filling in a gap in God's knowledge—it's a tool to gauge how His grace is growing in your life.

When God asks you to do something, there's always a point. Take Acts 12:5, for example. Peter was in prison. The church didn't just say, "What a shame." Instead, they cared enough about him to speak to God on Peter's behalf.

The alternative to this kind of compassion is the trend of sending positive vibes. This only says, "I'm thinking about your struggle." Intercession, however, says, "I care enough about you that I am asking God to help you."

Intercession will always have the greatest impact.

» THINK ABOUT IT

- Why does sending vibes fall short of God's instructions?
- How can intercession improve your ability to empathize with others?
- When is a good time to intercede for others?

» PRAY ABOUT IT

- Ask God to help you notice people's struggles.
- Let your sadness for another's loss move you to pray.
- Determine that intercession is the perfect way to stand with others.

People struggle every day, God.
Help me care enough to intercede on
their behalf when I talk to You.

33. Pleading in Prayer

[Jesus said,] "I have pleaded in prayer for you, Simon, that your faith should not fail. So when you have repented and turned to me again, strengthen your brothers."

LUKE 22:32 NLT

If you want someone to pray for you, there's no one better than Jesus. Simon (also known as Peter) had just heard Jesus say that Simon's best would not be good enough. His intentions were good, but his promise-keeping abilities were broken. He would deny that he knew Jesus and run away when Jesus was arrested. But Jesus interceded for this impulsive disciple, following up this seeming pronouncement of doom by saying that Peter would repent and turn toward Jesus. He would walk the path of the forgiven.

Like Peter, any broken man with failure in his past can take what he's learned and encourage other Christians. Every man needs to know he isn't alone.

Jesus sees the you that you could be, and His Spirit intercedes for you. He knows you'll fail and break your promises. But He wants you to feel absolutely comfortable in turning to Him so that you can encourage others who live with the same struggle.

» THINK ABOUT IT

- Why is it important to remember that everyone fails?

- How can failure help you seek God?

- How can you recognize God reaching out to you today?

» PRAY ABOUT IT

- Ask God's Spirit to pray for you.

- Recognize the God who makes success bloom in the soil of failure.

- Thank Him for your future. . .and dare to go there.

I want Your Spirit to pray for me, Father.
You know the best way to pray because
You know what You want me to be.

34. The Spirit's Prayer

*He that searcheth the hearts knoweth
what is the mind of the Spirit, because
he maketh intercession for the saints
according to the will of God.*
ROMANS 8:27 KJV

This is another case study of how God's Spirit prays for you. *But if God's Spirit is God,* you might be thinking, *why would He pray to God for me?* Well, the way God does things isn't the way you do things. What makes sense to Him may be confusing to you. Maybe the real question is this: Are you okay with God praying for you?

One key point to Romans 8:27 is that when God's Spirit prays for you, He doesn't necessarily champion your position. Rather, He prays "according to the will of God." His prayer won't be selfish, uninformed, or confused. God's Spirit knows what you need, so He won't ask God for anything He already knows will receive a negative reply.

God's wisdom is found in His Spirit's interceding prayer. You'll never have a greater prayer offered on your behalf.

» THINK ABOUT IT

- Why can't God's Spirit pray a selfish prayer?
- How should you respond to His prayer? Why?
- How can you trust the Spirit to pray for what you need?

» PRAY ABOUT IT

- Trust God's Spirit enough to welcome His prayer.
- Ask for God's intervention so that you can find the help you need.
- Pay attention to the things God says yes to.

Would Your Spirit pray for me, Lord? Step in and change my heart when it doesn't match Your will.

35. The One with Authority

I urge, then, first of all, that petitions, prayers, intercession and thanksgiving be made for all people—for kings and all those in authority.
1 TIMOTHY 2:1–2 NIV

Petitions, *prayers*, *intercession*, and *thanksgiving* may sound like nice and biblical words, but what exactly do they mean?

A petition recognizes God's authority to answer requests, a prayer is a request made to this authority, intercession is a prayer on behalf of someone who needs God's help, and thanksgiving is an expression of gratitude for when God hears the other three.

If God didn't have the power to help, why would you pray to Him? And if He couldn't help you, then why would you suppose He could help others? And if He couldn't answer prayers, what use would you have for thankfulness?

You pray because you believe that He's able and willing to help. Then you can come boldly to the greatest authority in the universe and make requests—not just for yourself but for kings, leaders, neighbors, family, and friends.

» THINK ABOUT IT

- Why is it important to believe that God has authority over all things?

- What is the difference between petitions and intercession?

- How can your prayer influence other people?

» PRAY ABOUT IT

- Tell God that you recognize and accept His authority.

- Ask God for help and wait patiently to see His answer unfold.

- Be grateful because a good God with supreme authority listens to you.

There is nothing that You can't control, God. I need help, and only You can help me. Thank You for listening to me and working for my good.

36. Mercy Improved

There is one God and one Mediator
who can reconcile God and humanity—
the man Christ Jesus.
1 TIMOTHY 2:5 NLT

The following illustration isn't new, but it might help you understand what happens when Jesus intercedes (mediates) for you.

Imagine God as a judge before whom you are compelled to stand trial. You're guilty of breaking His law, and He doesn't need a prosecutor—He's intimately aware of your sin. All He has to do is pronounce judgment. You, however, need a defender. *That's Jesus.*

Jesus represents you before His Father. You have a legal advocate, and He has a perfect track record. This staying hand of defense doesn't diminish justice—it improves the response of mercy. He's not interested in attaching some underlying motive to your disobedience; there's no excuse or loophole that will ever work as a defense. Rather, Jesus stands before God and says, "Yes, he is guilty, but when I died on the cross, I paid the price for his sin."

This single bit of jurisprudence in spiritual law is the sum total of your defense—and it works every time. *Not guilty.*

» THINK ABOUT IT

- Why should the idea of Jesus as defender improve your understanding of God's mercy?

- How does this picture challenge your idea of trying to please God on your own?

- What does it mean to be represented by Jesus?

» PRAY ABOUT IT

- Don't be afraid to ask for Jesus to be your mediator.

- Admit your guilt.

- Be ready to accept forgiveness.

---

*I stand guilty before You, Father.
I ask Jesus to offer proof that the
price for my sin has been paid.*

37. Interceding for All

[Jesus said,] "You have heard that it was said, 'Love your neighbor and hate your enemy.' But I tell you, love your enemies and pray for those who persecute you."
MATTHEW 5:43–44 NIV

Today's passage is probably familiar to you. You might even see it regularly paraphrased on social media. However, a much different attitude seems to be gaining traction—one that suggests you shouldn't let a "toxic" person back into your life. The end result of these thoughts is essentially that you shouldn't forgive but hold grudges instead. When you put it that way, it somehow sounds less right.

Jesus' instruction sounds nothing like this. He says you are to do better things for enemies than they have ever done for you. Then you are to go even further by bringing their needs to Him in prayer. It's hard to speak badly about people when you're praying for them! This greatly differs from the modern tendency to dismiss those who don't seem to have time for you.

By following these instructions, you can intercede for anyone you encounter. . .no matter how that encounter ended.

» THINK ABOUT IT

- Is it challenging for you to pray for those who've hurt you?
- Why is it easier to hold a grudge than to love?
- Is anything preventing you from following God's instructions?

» PRAY ABOUT IT

- Ask for strength to love and pray for disagreeable people.
- Ask for insight on how obeying these instructions will help you.
- Agree to God's plan and refuse to let your personal opinions change your mind.

I admit it is hard to pray for some people, Lord. For them, I want justice; for me, I want mercy. Help me remember that You ask me to do for them what You did for me.

38. Jeopardy

*I sought for a man among them, that
should make up the hedge, and stand
in the gap before me for the land, that I
should not destroy it: but I found none.*

EZEKIEL 22:30 KJV

An army looks for a way into the enemy camp. If they can find an opening, victory is all but certain.

God is asking you to protect an area from the enemy and report to Him anything you feel is important. In Ezekiel 22, God wanted someone to intercede for the people, to alert the people to danger, and to stand in the gap between His protection and their demise. He was looking for an unselfish person who would put the needs of the people before personal comfort or amusement. God looked, but sadly. . .God just couldn't find.

It was as though the people had said, "We just don't care anymore. The land is Yours to destroy." Who does that? When you refuse to intercede, this is what your actions proclaim. When you learn to care for other people by interceding for them in prayer, you are showing compassion for the entire body of Christ—when one person is in jeopardy, so is everyone else.

» THINK ABOUT IT

- Why is it so easy to wait for someone else to stand in the gap and intercede?

- Why is it important that you be the one who intercedes?

- How will you stand in the gap today?

» PRAY ABOUT IT

- Intercede for your family, city, and country.

- Ask for wisdom to know for whom you should intercede.

- Seek to be a leader and obey God's calling.

---

*Help me stand between destruction and
Your help, God. May my willingness to
intercede match Your willingness to help.*

39. Get Tough on Pride

*Confess your sins to each other and pray for
each other so that you may be healed. The
earnest prayer of a righteous person has great
power and produces wonderful results.*

JAMES 5:16 NLT

God has no use for pride, and He hates it when you use it
to seek admiration. However, it's hard to hold on to pride
whenever you're constantly owning up to your mistakes.
Confessing your sins to other people keeps you account-
able. . .and keeps pride at a minimum.

There's something healing about refusing to believe you're
better than others. But transparency can be especially hard
if you're trying to hide poor choices from people who expect
better from you. You might feel the need to conceal your sin
rather than disappoint the people you love. But God's plan is
for you to be as free in admitting sin to others as you should
be admitting sin to Him.

If you can be that transparent with others and with God,
then there's nothing hidden when you pray. This is when
effective prayer happens—when you don't have to hold
back because you aren't distracted by unconfessed sin. Your
prayer life will have more meaning when you admit each sin
as soon as it happens.

» THINK ABOUT IT

- When was the last time you confessed to anyone that you sinned?

- How can you make this hard task easier?

- What are some of the benefits of confessing sin?

» PRAY ABOUT IT

- Thank God for the courage He can bring to you in confessing sin.

- Ask God to help you be transparent with people about your struggle.

- Don't hinder your prayer life by hiding your sin.

Make me brave enough to admit when I do wrong, Father. Help others forgive me and still love me. I don't want to hide the man You're transforming.

40. A Failure to Pray

"As for me, far be it from me that I should sin against the LORD by failing to pray for you."
1 SAMUEL 12:23 NIV

Interceding for others is not just a good idea that you can practice whenever you feel like it. No, God wants followers who are all in.

The prophet Samuel said he would be breaking God's law if he failed to pray for the people whom he'd been sent to help. He had a message, but he knew that only God could give them the wisdom they needed in order to hear it.

Your prayer for others can show a compassion that reaches beyond giving money, lending physical help, or speaking kind words. Any of these three without prayer is still not enough. Prayer without one of these other three, however, may not be God's best. Your personal involvement and willingness to bring God to the struggle indicates a deep compassion.

When you see that someone has a need, never leave God out of the solution. Pray.

» THINK ABOUT IT

- Why do you think Samuel felt prayer was so important that he considered it sin not to pray?

- Have you ever considered praying for others a very good option. . .but stopped short of doing it?

- When does God want you all in? Why?

» PRAY ABOUT IT

- Bring compassion with you when you pray.

- Mix prayer with your willingness to help.

- Ask God to do what you cannot for others.

I want to be compassionate in both my words and actions, Lord. May what I say to You invite Your compassion to people I care about.

41. Applications in Intercession

Moses cried unto the LORD, saying, Heal her now, O God, I beseech thee.

NUMBERS 12:13 KJV

It was a time of infighting in the wandering camp of Israel. Moses was leading because God called him to lead. Whether it was sibling rivalry or adult jealousy, Moses' brother, Aaron, and sister, Miriam, began privately discussing their growing disdain for their younger brother's seeming privilege. This point was brought out into the open, and Moses was challenged by his own family.

God brought swift justice. Miriam stood accused, and she was judged quickly. Her sentence? Leprosy—a horrible skin disease. The judgment was appropriate, given the circumstances, but it was too much for Moses. So this leader, whom God had just defended against unjust accusations, began interceding for Miriam, begging God to heal her.

Moses knew God was displeased with Miriam's decisions, but he was still bold enough to approach God to ask for mercy. God answered his prayer.

Chances are, you've probably had a few Miriams in your life—people who have treated you harshly but are now being humiliated themselves. If so, do as Moses did. Intercede.

» THINK ABOUT IT

- Why should you want to have someone interceding for you when you sin?

- What struck you the most about this story? Why?

- How can interceding for others bring mercy when judgment is expected?

» PRAY ABOUT IT

- Be bold enough to ask for God's mercy.

- Be honorable enough to pray, even when it seems someone is getting what they deserve.

- Be compassionate and loving enough to intercede.

Your mercy is important, God. So is Your judgment. Help me find the courage to pray for kindness in another's life, even when it may not seem that they deserve it.

42. The Tears of Interceding Prayer

Tears stream from my eyes because of the destruction of my people! My tears flow endlessly; they will not stop until the LORD looks down from heaven and sees.
LAMENTATIONS 3:48–50 NLT

Jeremiah wasn't called "the weeping prophet" without reason. One of the primary ways people demonstrate their inward pain and sorrow is by crying. And because Jeremiah deeply felt the loss of his nation's soul, his cheeks and face were stained with tears.

Lamentations 3 suggests that God recognizes tears in the same way He recognizes prayers. Jeremiah's tears seemed to be a form of prayer: when he had no words, he cried. And in his sorrow, God heard his heart's request.

The people of Israel were experiencing destruction, bringing Jeremiah to a place of empathy and compassion. He felt the sorrow the people felt, and his tears acted as a wordless prayer that cried, "God, please help us."

Being emotional in prayer isn't a weakness—it's the result of being connected to other humans. When you intercede for other people, you feel the burdens they carry. And if that makes you emotional, just remember: the prophet Jeremiah chose tears as a form of interceding prayer.

» THINK ABOUT IT

- When you pray, do you sometimes think emotions are off limits?
- How does it help knowing that Jeremiah felt such profound sorrow for his nation?
- How can freedom in your emotional response change the way you pray?

» PRAY ABOUT IT

- Thank God for the ability to pray emotionally.
- Allow His wisdom to calm you.
- Accept His help as joy replaces sorrow.

I'm not always in a good mood, Father. Thanks for hearing me when I pray. I look forward to joy and a decrease in sorrow.

43. The Family Care Cast

Casting all your care upon him;
for he careth for you.
1 PETER 5:7 KJV

Maybe your teen child is out too late, keeping secrets and being disrespectful. Perhaps your spouse is having health issues, job difficulties, or a bout with depression. Whatever it is, you're facing your own struggles, and you're doing your best to keep everything together. It isn't easy, and you're not sure you can hold on. Some days, you're certain you can't.

And you're right—your family burdens are bigger than your ability to manage them. So relieve the pressure by letting God take *everything*, not just what you're willing to give up. Even if you think you can manage something on your own, you'll never manage it better than He can.

You and your family need help that can only come from the compassionate heart of God. Because He cares, you don't have to live with an anxious heart. He doesn't do this because you deserve it or because He "owes you one"; rather, He does this because He loves you and cares deeply for you.

On the bad days—and the good ones too—remember that God cares for your family even more than you do.

» THINK ABOUT IT

- Have you ever felt hopeless when it comes to your family?

- What have you done to manage the stress associated with compassionately caring for your family?

- Why do you think God cares so much for your family?

» PRAY ABOUT IT

- Thank God for permission to cast your cares.

- Ask Him to remind you of things you should be casting in His direction.

- Tell your family to welcome God into their struggles.

I want You to know that I'm grateful, Lord.
The fact that You share my struggles
keeps me from being overwhelmed.

44. Build Each Other Up

*Encourage one another and build each
other up, just as in fact you are doing.*
1 THESSALONIANS 5:11 NIV

Have you ever thought of praying with your family as a way to encourage them? There's not a bundle of flowers, new toy, or expensive supper that can mean more than the prayers you offer for your family when you speak to the God who listens.

God recognizes this next-level compassion when your family members find their way into your prayers. This isn't a test or God's way of grading you; rather, it's a matter of whatever means the most to you naturally becoming a part of your conversations with God. Pray for them privately. Pray for them in their presence. Pray for them every chance you get, remembering how much God wants to impact their lives.

The greatest difficulties become lighter with each prayer. God made family relationships to be the most powerful human connections that exist; therefore, it's only natural that you address your family's issues to the God who has answers. This encouragement is one way God can bring the members of your family together.

» THINK ABOUT IT

- How might you use prayer to encourage your family?
- What are some ongoing needs for your family?
- How can prayer bring your family closer?

» PRAY ABOUT IT

- Take requests from your family and commit to sharing them with God.
- Find a way to remember to pray for your family.
- Ask God for family blessings, unity, and help.

My family is important to me, God. When they are concerned, help me pay attention and encourage them through prayer.

45. A Family Blessing

*"I entrust you to God and the message
of his grace that is able to build you up
and give you an inheritance with all
those he has set apart for himself."*
ACTS 20:32 NLT

Have you ever prayed a blessing for any member of your family? If not, you should give it a try. It costs nothing, but it changes a lot.

Seek to identify God's dream for your family and then let that inform your prayer of blessing for them. The blessing might have a greater impact if you personally pray with each family member.

Reread Acts 20:32 and imagine saying this to someone in your family. Then adapt this passage to something that sounds more personal. This might look like, "I can't take care of you the way God can, so I've asked Him to watch over you. May His undeserved blessings encourage you so that when you accept His rescue, you gain heaven as your destination. May you always have a purpose and remain effective in serving God."

And finally, after this blessing, send a prayer asking God to make it true.

» THINK ABOUT IT

- Do you feel inspired to bless a family member?
- How do you think a blessing would encourage them?
- Why would a blessing from you be a pleasant surprise to a loved one?

» PRAY ABOUT IT

- Ask God to help you bless someone.
- Write down your blessing to remember what you want to say.
- Pray for the strength to say what needs to be said.

Father, I'm not sure I feel comfortable blessing a family member; it sounds awkward. But You have blessed me, so help me bless the ones I love.

46. Be the Example

*Train up a child in the way he should go: and
when he is old, he will not depart from it.*
PROVERBS 22:6 KJV

Does your family know that you pray? Or have you kept it
a secret? You don't have to stand on a kitchen chair with
a megaphone, shouting spiritual words for all to hear—it's
quite possible that the majority of your prayers are quiet and
solitary. But does your family know that prayer is important
to you? Have they learned that you are praying for them and
asking God to intervene?

If you want your children to be praying Christians, they'll
need to see you do it first. It's much harder when you adopt
a "do as I say and not as I do" attitude. You may want your
child to follow God's example, but do they have the benefit
of seeing you do the same? Children trust their parents first,
and that trust should serve as a prime encouragement to
trust God.

You can teach them all you want about the importance of
following God, but examples always speak louder than words.

» THINK ABOUT IT

- Why is setting a good example important to your family?

- How can your example encourage your children to follow God?

- Are you motivated to trust God and follow through on His plan?

» PRAY ABOUT IT

- Ask God to help you make prayer a daily choice.

- Set aside time every day to have a conversation with God.

- Thank God for His patience.

It seems prayer is about more than asking for help, Lord. May I be motivated to pray in a way that sets an example for my family.

47. The Ones Who Came Before

My son, keep your father's command and
do not forsake your mother's teaching.

PROVERBS 6:20 NIV

If you're reading this, then you're likely an adult male. (That's who this book was written for, after all!)

Maybe you had fantastic parents. If so, great! Show your respect by praying for them. Prayer, in fact, can be the personal proof of your love.

Or maybe you left an abusive home to begin life as an adult. Perhaps you have some deep resentment toward your parents. Maybe you and your family have some dark skeletons in the closet. Not all family units are storybook material. Happy endings are for fairy tales—emotional pain often resonates more with reality.

When you pray for your family, extend your prayer beyond your spouse and children and include your parents as well. They shouldn't be set aside because of their poor decisions or lack of influence over your life. Shutting your parents out will only nurture your pain until you finally forgive.

Pray for those who come after you, but also pray for those who came before. It's an act of love, respect, and honor.

» THINK ABOUT IT

- How can respecting your parents improve other relationships?

- Why is parental respect so important to God?

- Besides prayer, what other ways can you show your parents respect?

» PRAY ABOUT IT

- Thank God for your parents.

- Ask God to help you see your parents through the lens of compassion.

- Pray to be an example for your children, who will one day be adults.

---

*Help me show love to my parents by asking
You to bless them, Father. My choice can
be a teacher to my own children.*

48. An Outsider's Example

He was a devout, God-fearing man, as was
everyone in his household. He gave generously
to the poor and prayed regularly to God.
Acts 10:2 nlt

Cornelius was a surprising example of a praying man. He was a Roman soldier, and his subjects followed God and prayed to Him. Cornelius did as well. In fact, his entire household loved God.

Instead of making things hard for the poor, Cornelius did something unexpected: he financially assisted them. Consequently, he set an example not only for his family but for anyone who hadn't yet chosen to follow God.

You can't control which family you were born into, but you do get to choose whom you'll follow. Cornelius—an outsider who worked for the people the Jews considered an enemy—chose to follow God, making Him a priority in his family. In turn, his family made God a priority in their lives too. So when the gospel came to him, he gladly accepted.

Through the life of this outsider, God taught new lessons to His people.

» THINK ABOUT IT

- Why is it important that the Jews considered Cornelius an outsider?

- How can you identify with Cornelius?

- What parts of this story give you hope?

» PRAY ABOUT IT

- Admit to God that you're an outsider.

- Thank Him that He loves outsiders.

- Ask Him to help you be a godly example in your own family.

God, thank You for loving me, going out of Your way to find me, and adopting me. Help my family see You in me and choose to walk with us.

49. Good Things Waiting

Set your affection on things above,
not on things on the earth.
Colossians 3:2 KJV

Not all things are created equal. You may want a new UTV, for instance, but you'd never need it as much as you need forgiveness. A paid trip to a championship football game would be amazing, but it could never compete with God's rescue plan.

Every Christian man agrees with these truths, yet we often get more excited about the four-wheeler or game ticket than we do about salvation. That's perhaps because the things you should long for the most aren't physically here—they are with God, waiting for your arrival. But even if you have to wait awhile to interact with them, these God-given gifts are yours just the same.

When you pray, think of your future in heaven—a perfect, sorrow-free place where games and off-roading won't matter. This is a once-in-an-eternity event, and it's what you should be longing for.

Today, tell God how excited you are about heaven. Then get your family in on the excitement. As you talk about God's future, imagine what good things are waiting.

» THINK ABOUT IT

- Do you need to go back to the basics of God's plan for you?

- What temporary good things might you need to replace with God's great future?

- How can you help your family experience the joy of this anticipation?

» PRAY ABOUT IT

- Try to remember God's future more than any other event.

- Confess when other things become more important to you.

- Thank God for a future that you can be a part of.

My future with You is going to be amazing, Lord. I forget sometimes, so help me remember to look forward to seeing You.

50. Adoption

"I will be your Father, and you will be my sons and daughters, says the LORD Almighty."

2 CORINTHIANS 6:18 NLT

God asks you to recognize the difference between yourself and unbelievers. He calls you to be separate, distinct, and original. Your new identity was born when you allowed God to work in your life. Others, however, often offer a stiff arm, making sure God understands He's not welcome in their affairs.

When you accept rescue, you become one of God's sons and He becomes your Father. Those who don't know God cannot empathize with you, but they can and will strategize against you. They are children of someone else. . .and he's never been a great parent. They can accept rescue and become adopted as well, so they are never lost causes; however, if you befriend them, they will bring the influence of their father, Satan, to the table. By praying to the Father of your spiritual family, you can keep your new life moving in a better direction.

You're welcome in God's family because He welcomes all who come to Him. But don't be surprised when your friends examine His offer and say, "No thanks." Just remember to pray for them while you return to your Father's side.

THINK ABOUT IT

- What are some of the benefits of being adopted by God?

- What does being called a son of God mean to you?

- How does your adopted status challenge other relationships?

PRAY ABOUT IT

- Thank God for adopting you.

- Ask for the courage to tell people about your Father.

- Admit that it may be difficult to always choose God first.

I'm so glad to be part of Your family, Father. Help me use prayer to share my struggle and pray for people who need to be adopted too.

51. Born in a Battle Zone

*Do not conform to the pattern of this world, but
be transformed by the renewing of your mind.
Then you will be able to test and approve what
God's will is—his good, pleasing and perfect will.*
ROMANS 12:2 NIV

You were born in a battle zone. It may not have seemed like it—pictures show you in a hospital or in your mother's arms—but it was a battle zone nonetheless. Ideas, some good and some diabolical, soon began vying for your allegiance.

Your parents might've done their best to protect their children from harmful ideas, but the more independence you gained, the more these ideas were introduced. The battle that's waged since the beginning of time caught up to you. Now, you observe this battle every day.

God encourages His soldiers to stand firm, refuse to conform, and allow Him to transform how and what they think. You'll fully realize the value of these exceptional instructions only when you internalize and follow them.

One way you can accomplish God's perfect will is by praying for clarification on how to take His instructions into the workplace, among your peers, and in the company of strangers.

Pray—read—obey—repeat.

» THINK ABOUT IT

- How is it helpful to think of culture as a battle zone?

- Why would it be wrong to assume people, not bad ideas, are the enemy?

- What clarification from God would be helpful in making transformational choices?

» PRAY ABOUT IT

- Admit that some battles are hard to fight.

- Confess the times when you've chosen the wrong ideas.

- Ask for wisdom to know what to believe and how to act on that belief.

I'm not always fit for battle, God. I need to accept Your help and discover a soldier's courage.

52. Boundaries Removed

There is no longer Jew or Gentile,
slave or free, male and female.
For you are all one in Christ Jesus.
GALATIANS 3:28 NLT

You don't belong to a club, a clique, or a fraternity. As a Christian, you've always belonged to a family. It doesn't matter where you were born, how much money you make, or the color of your skin. Language, geographical, or social barriers don't exist when it comes to prayer.

You can pray with and find compassion toward people who live outside of your typical sphere of influence. Even more, you can actually love people you've never met. God is always working with His children to remove barriers between people and His love.

When you view any group as superior (or inferior) to another, you miss God's message. He loved all, sent Jesus to rescue the willing, and gently directs the seeker to Himself. When you want to know more, He wants to help you understand.

God is willing to accept all, and He wants you to do the same. This means refusing to compromise the message yet accepting anyone who will listen to God's good news.

THINK ABOUT IT

- Why is it important to note that God chose all humans, not a specific "group," to love?

- What can you do to adopt God's view of people?

- How might this challenge your worldview?

 PRAY ABOUT IT

- Admit God's love is unlimited.

- Admit His truth is unchangeable.

- Confess any exclusions you might've made.

Help me catch a vision for Your deep and impressive love, Lord. Help me never restrict anyone who needs to know You.

53. The World You Live In

*Love not the world, neither the things that
are in the world. If any man love the world,
the love of the Father is not in him.*

1 JOHN 2:15 KJV

You live in a culture that loves both the bright and shiny as well as the dark and deviant. All are designed to distract you from what matters most.

If you are won over by the bright and shiny, it will keep you away from God's best. If that doesn't work, more subversive options are available. But bad decisions don't always have a noticeable cause. Sometimes, they're prompted by simply not doing the right thing.

You don't have to do something despicable to get off track. You might lose your way by refusing to help someone else. You may not be doing anything you think of as wrong, but you're also not doing anything God can use to bring His plan to life for anyone else. If your enemy wanted to derail you, convincing you to choose nothing would be enough.

That's why you need prayer—it keeps you in contact with God, who has the perfect plan and sees the big picture.

In His love, God sends you opportunities to do something good. . .and He never stops.

THINK ABOUT IT

- Why might doing nothing cause you to fall away from God's plan?

- How can prayer keep you from doing nothing?

- When can you start?

PRAY ABOUT IT

- Admit that you don't always do what you know you should.

- Ask God to help you see that His love for people requires action.

- Take the time to pray because it offers purpose to today's plans.

Sometimes, I'm pretty good at doing nothing, Father. Help me use the purpose You've given me to do good for people You love.

54. Wiser Than

Whenever the king consulted them in any matter requiring wisdom and balanced judgment, he found them ten times more capable than any of the magicians and enchanters in his entire kingdom.
DANIEL 1:20 NLT

You may be familiar with Daniel's story. If not, here's the quick summary: Daniel and a few young men his age were taken captive to Babylon. They loved God and followed Him faithfully. But something about them stood out to the king—as capable as the king's magicians and enchanters were, they could not compare to the wisdom of Daniel and his friends.

These youths were thrust into a new culture, given new names, and forced to leave their families and their homes. But rather than feeling like victims, they boldly chose to do something more with their difficult position: they followed the king's orders. . .except when he asked them to break God's law. Because they chose not to compromise just to avoid negative attention, even the king eventually saw their wisdom.

You have that same opportunity every day. You don't have to "go along to get along." You can stand for something important and leave the results to God—only He can close the lions' mouths and quench the flames.

» THINK ABOUT IT

- What makes compromise so appealing?
- How can prayer make compromise less appealing?
- How can you trust God by making hard decisions?

» PRAY ABOUT IT

- Ask God to help you avoid compromise when His laws are clear.
- Use prayer to keep you centered on God's plan.
- Thank God for the clarity found in His Word.

I don't want to compromise when You've given a command, God. Keep me linked to Your plan and help me understand what You've asked.

55. Cultural Guesses

*See to it that no one takes you captive through
hollow and deceptive philosophy, which depends
on human tradition and the elemental spiritual
forces of this world rather than on Christ.*
Colossians 2:8 niv

The court of public opinion is enormous and fickle. The line between right and wrong shifts like a sidewinder snake in the sand. People will spout ideas, insisting everything they say is true, and then change their mind when a new theory strikes their fancy. They then forget what they told you last time. . .and hope you'll do the same.

The role of these conflicting beliefs is to bring chaos to the hearts of millions. If you read a broad section of news, you'll discover that aspirin is good—and bad—for you, that eating carbs is the way your body creates energy—and you should avoid it. It all depends on what source you believe.

In the Christian life, you already have an impeccable source for truth. God's Word dispels rumors, refutes lies, and controls chaos. Your prayer can take culture's worst and recast its philosophies as either fact or fiction.

How? God gives wisdom where culture can only guess.

» THINK ABOUT IT

- Do you ever see people's guesses as more interesting than God's truth?

- How can you learn to tell the difference between guesses and truth?

- Why is it important to know the difference?

» PRAY ABOUT IT

- Admit that you've believed lies.

- Read the Bible to learn truth.

- Ask God to help you stop guessing.

Lord, sometimes I believe a lie without asking You for the truth. May I never believe or share anything You say isn't true.

56. Faith Defender

Let your speech be always with grace,
seasoned with salt, that ye may know
how ye ought to answer every man.
COLOSSIANS 4:6 KJV

When you are fully acquainted with God and comfortable talking to Him, you can become better at talking with people about Him. Your conversations with God can overflow into your everyday conversations. Your words can be the perfect seasoning that increases the spiritual hunger of others.

People are seeking answers, and many Christians respond in an unhelpful way. That can lead seekers to believe that either you don't know God or He's not that important to you. And if He's not important to you, then why should God be important to them? If you're supposed to know Him and yet you have no answers, then maybe God can't be known.

That's not true, of course, but your actions—or inactions—might give that impression. To engage culture, you need to know God and be willing to represent Him to anyone who asks you to defend your faith.

Because you care about others, it just makes sense to know more about God. People want to know more about God, and they want to learn more from someone they trust.

Can they trust you?

THINK ABOUT IT

- Why do your words matter to anyone who hears you?

- How can prayer equip you to represent God?

- What does caring about others have to do with prayer?

PRAY ABOUT IT

- Admit that you need to stay close to God.

- Commit to representing God to others.

- Ask for help in speaking the words others need to hear.

---

*Being close to You is both personal
and practical, Father. Help others hear
the words You want me to speak.*

57. God's Word Inspires

*Keep on loving each other as brothers and
sisters. Don't forget to show hospitality to
strangers, for some who have done this
have entertained angels without realizing it!
Remember those in prison, as if you were there
yourself. Remember also those being mistreated,
as if you felt their pain in your own bodies.*
HEBREWS 13:1-3 NLT

Take Hebrews 13:1–3 and turn it into a prayer for your culture. Maybe it'll look something like this: "Lord, help me love other people as if they were family. There are men and women in prison, many of whom have families and friends that they miss. There are other people who are hurting while I'm talking to You. If I were in their place, it would seem very hard. But I don't have to be in their shoes to understand that life hurts and that only You can remove the pain. Help me take every opportunity to show kindness through hospitality. Everyone I assist is someone You created. Help the displaced and hurting and give me the chance to share what I know about You."

This is something anybody can do. By making God's Word a part of your prayer experience, you can let God know that you're paying attention to Him and the people He made.

» THINK ABOUT IT

- How can restating biblical truth in your prayers show God you're paying attention?

- What can biblical prayers do to impact the world around you?

- Why does God believe your involvement in the lives of others matters?

» PRAY ABOUT IT

- Take a passage of scripture and use it to inspire a personal prayer.

- Ask God to help you understand His Word so well that you can make it a prayer.

- Thank God for the beauty of meaningful words.

May my prayers show that I'm paying attention to what You say, God. Give me the wisdom to learn what You mean.

58. Be a Direction Giver

I am not ashamed of the gospel, because it is the power of God that brings salvation to everyone who believes.

ROMANS 1:16 NIV

People need God. That's probably evident when you read the news or even drive around town. But it's evident in your family too, and you probably recognize the need even in your own life.

Society needs God, even when they won't admit it. They're like men who refuse to ask for directions, choosing to waste time and gas instead. People who don't know God keep searching, either refusing to ask for direction or heeding the wrong advice.

We as Christians don't have to wait for someone to ask us how to find God—we should always be ready to pass on the needed intel, eager and unashamed. People need help, and we're the ones who can offer it.

God instructs you on how to live, but He also asks you to share what you're learning—no fear, embarrassment, or apology. The news you can share is life changing. You just need the "want to."

» THINK ABOUT IT

- Why does it make no sense to be ashamed of God?
- How can you use what you know about God to help someone today?
- What is the main benefit of sharing the way to find God?

» PRAY ABOUT IT

- Ask for help in learning directions so that you can share directions.
- Admit that it's sometimes hard to share.
- Ask God to help those who have yet to walk His way.

Help me learn Your way so that I can show Your way, Lord. Even when it's hard, help me share what I know about You so that others have the chance to follow You too.

59. The Language You Use

When we tell you these things, we do not use words that come from human wisdom. Instead, we speak words given to us by the Spirit, using the Spirit's words to explain spiritual truths.
1 CORINTHIANS 2:13 NLT

Some people refer to the language of Christians as *Christianese*. When Christians use terms they find in scripture, the culture at large often struggles to understand.

When you say things like "blood of the Lamb," "quiet time," or "hedge of protection," you'll likely get some pretty strange looks from outsiders. You might feel comfortable with the terminology, but you may need to ask God for some help in explaining it to others.

Although you have God's Spirit to help you understand, the one who doesn't follow God has no such translation service, which is why it can be helpful to take the time to explain. That's why God clearly says you should be ready to give a defense of your faith by explaining what you know about God.

Prayer enhances your ability to understand what God is saying when you read the instructions in His book.

» THINK ABOUT IT

- Why is it important to learn the language of Christianity?

- How can knowing what God wants help you explain it to others?

- What can you do to improve translation services when you talk to others about God?

» PRAY ABOUT IT

- Ask God to teach you what He wants from you.

- Invest time in making what you know understandable.

- Pray that God would give you opportunity to share with others in words they will understand.

You have instructions You need me to understand, Father. Once I understand, help me help others understand the same thing.

60. No Better—No Worse

*Suppose a man comes into your meeting
wearing a gold ring and fine clothes, and
a poor man in filthy old clothes also comes
in. If you show special attention to the man
wearing fine clothes and say, "Here's a good
seat for you," but say to the poor man, "You
stand there" or "Sit on the floor by my feet,"
have you not discriminated among yourselves
and become judges with evil thoughts?*
JAMES 2:2–4 NIV

You've probably heard the expression, "Money makes the world go round." As definitive as that sounds, money has no power greater than what you give it.

Don't offer money more strength than it deserves. When you give it the ability to influence, it makes you do crazy things, like discriminating against the poor. God never did that, and He doesn't now.

Also, don't allow money to be your primary test for honor. Rich people with unlimited resources are no better or worse than poor people with none, so don't treat them as such. If you do, you're assigning value to something God might condemn. Pride, after all, is money's closest companion.

» THINK ABOUT IT

- How can money influence how people treat others?
- Why is money a faulty test for true worth?
- What can you do to resist making money a priority in your relationships?

» PRAY ABOUT IT

- Confess if you have made money too important.
- Admit you are willing to change your thinking.
- Ask God for a more correct way to see others.

God, help me see people and not the things they own. Help me love others with no questions about their bank account.

61. He's No Slacker

*The Lord is not slack concerning his promise, as
some men count slackness; but is longsuffering
to us-ward, not willing that any should perish,
but that all should come to repentance.*
2 PETER 3:9 KJV

The word *slacker* doesn't apply to God in any way. He doesn't shirk responsibility, and He isn't slow—He's always on time. He never gets frustrated if you think He's taking too long to fulfill His promises, and He doesn't respond to your impatience.

No, that's not God. Your timing may be very different from His, but His is always superior.

In the one area where no one wants God to be hasty—His judgment—He's described as patient. He wants everyone to accept His gift of rescue. So if He seems slow, then remember: it's simply controlled patience. He's actually waiting to celebrate a sinner's rescue. This too should be something you pray for.

God wants to find the lost, forgive sinners, and heal hurting hearts. If He decides to be patient while people wrestle with accepting His rescue, then why would we ever complain?

So pray, knowing that God will never be late—even if it seems that way to you.

» THINK ABOUT IT

- Why is God patient with stubborn people?
- Why might some people be hesitant about God's rescue?
- How long is too long for God to wait for someone to repent? Why?

» PRAY ABOUT IT

- Admit that you are sometimes impatient.
- Pray that people will see their need for rescue.
- Praise God for refusing to give up easily on people.

When I'm impatient, Lord, remind me that You're giving people time to find You.

62. Only God Can Do That

God saved you by his grace when you believed. And you can't take credit for this; it is a gift from God. Salvation is not a reward for the good things we have done, so none of us can boast about it.

EPHESIANS 2:8-9 NLT

Taking credit for good deeds may require a rethink. Who's teaching you? Who forgave you? Who is helping you? This isn't self-help—it's God's help. This isn't a place for personal pride—it's God's all-expenses-paid rescue of a law breaker.

People who are lost need to be found—and the found don't need to shout their good deeds. The only name that should be honored is God's.

Pray for the opportunity to share God with others, and pray for those who need to know God. They don't need you to take credit for the good things God has done for you.

God saves you because you can't save yourself. You need to embrace this truth if you want to understand just how amazing His gift is. Boasting about something you didn't do is equal to telling people they can rescue themselves—a dangerous lie. If they didn't need God's help, then Jesus' sacrifice would've been meaningless.

The found should give the lost a realistic picture of rescue: it comes only from God.

» THINK ABOUT IT

- Why would it be confusing and wrong to allow people to believe they can rescue themselves?

- How can pride mar your conversations about God?

- What can you do to keep God the focal point of your conversations?

» PRAY ABOUT IT

- Confess pride.

- Admit God rescues.

- Pray for the wisdom to witness humbly.

I've broken my best promise, Father. My efforts have never been good enough. Don't let me take credit for doing something only You can do.

63. God, the Seeker

The Son of man is come to seek and
to save that which was lost.
LUKE 19:10 KJV

God has no problem seeking lost people. Some want to be found, some don't know that they can be found, and some will try to hide as long as they can.

As believers, we too are seekers. God wants us to look for people who need Him and for ways to reach them. When that happens, we're simply doing what God has already been doing. He's just better at finding than we are.

God's kindness brings people out of their hiding spots and teaches them to trust Him. This knowledge then becomes a revelation of His goodness.

God knew that you would hide too. But His Son, Jesus, came to call the lost from their hiding spots—and He's patient in the waiting. He has so much to share, but still He waits for lost people to realize their need to be found.

The God who seeks is also the God who saves. He can do both, but not without the lost person's permission. We all must choose to be found.

» THINK ABOUT IT

- What does it mean to be sought by God?

- Why do people hesitate to be found?

- How can prayer link seekers with those who want to find?

» PRAY ABOUT IT

- Ask God to increase your concern for lost people.

- Make a list of people you'd love to see found.

- Ask God to allow you to encourage those being sought.

There are many people I would love to see found, God. I want people to see You in me so that maybe they'll choose to stop hiding.

64. They Don't Understand

*Satan, who is the god of this world, has
blinded the minds of those who don't believe.
They are unable to see the glorious light
of the Good News. They don't understand
this message about the glory of Christ,
who is the exact likeness of God.*

2 CORINTHIANS 4:4 NLT

God seeks so that He can save. Satan blinds to keep people hidden. God shows up, but they don't recognize Him. They hear His message, but it makes no sense.

God's message is clear, but if the one needing to be found has been paying attention to the one who blinds, then they'll walk away saying, "There's nothing to see here!"

One way you can pray for the lost is by praying that they'll not be blinded to God's presence by the enemy. Pray that they'll resist cynicism, consider the claims of God, and accept the saving work of Jesus.

Care enough about people that they become a regular part of your prayer life. God doesn't want you walking away from people who need Him simply because they don't have Him. He wants you to love such people. . .without doing anything to become like them. Satan would be happy to keep blinding anyone he can.

» THINK ABOUT IT

- Why is it disheartening that some people are blinded to God?

- Who would you most want to have a clear vision of God?

- How does the enemy use cynicism to distract the blinded?

» PRAY ABOUT IT

- Spend time thinking about the lost and fix their names in your mind.

- Ask God to make Himself known to them.

- Thank Him for improving the vision of the lost.

There are so many people who don't know You or believe You exist, Lord. Help them understand that You're real so that they can trust the new things they see.

65. God Sent You

*Praise be to the God and Father of our
Lord Jesus Christ, the Father of compassion
and the God of all comfort, who comforts
us in all our troubles, so that we can
comfort those in any trouble with the
comfort we ourselves receive from God.*
2 CORINTHIANS 1:3–4 NIV

How can you help the lost understand how good God is if you don't know how good He is either? How can you tell them that God offers comfort if you've never experienced it for yourself? All these claims would be true, but God wants you to experience His goodness—personally and often.

When you chose to believe God could rescue you, perhaps it was because you saw the way God impressively worked in the lives of believers. You could tell there was something different about them. . .and it was appealing.

You can pray for opportunities to show compassion, comfort those who hurt, and help those in need. After all, sharing facts about God will never impact anyone as much as sharing your personal testimony.

» THINK ABOUT IT

- Why would it be hard for others to recognize God's goodness in you if you can't recognize it yourself?

- How can God's comfort play a key role in sharing God's great rescue plan?

- What makes compassion so important in making God famous to others?

» PRAY ABOUT IT

- Confess that you don't always show compassion to others.

- Admit that God's plan is better than your actions.

- Ask God to populate your actions with His love.

I need to be compassionate, Father, but I sometimes fail. Your instructions are better than my actions. May what I do stem from Your love and not obligation.

66. The Finding

*What woman having ten pieces of silver, if she
lose one piece, doth not light a candle, and sweep
the house, and seek diligently till she find it?*

LUKE 15:8 KJV

It was just a story Jesus told, but this story teaches us an important truth: just as we don't stop seeking something valuable until we find it, God never stops seeking us.

Imagine a woman who has just enough money to pay her bills but then loses some of it. She retraces her steps, replays events in her mind, and probably prays for help. When she finds the money, she circles the neighborhood to recount this good news.

This short but brilliant story illustrates how important the lost are to God. He makes finding them a priority, and He rejoices when they're found. God's response should be your response as well.

The long-term lost aren't condemned for staying away so long. Instead, God rejoices when they finally understand and accept His rescue plan.

» THINK ABOUT IT

- Why do you think God makes such a big deal out of finding lost people?

- How can God's response become your response?

- When was the last time you rejoiced when someone discovered God's rescue?

» PRAY ABOUT IT

- Make a list of people you know have been rescued by God.

- Name them in prayer and rejoice with God that they have been found.

- Ask God to find more people so that you'll have a greater reason to rejoice.

I know people who have been found,
God, and I know many who are still lost.
I want to rejoice with You, and I can when
You find what You've been seeking.

67. Life Preserver

[Jesus] said to his disciples, "The harvest is great, but the workers are few. So pray to the Lord who is in charge of the harvest; ask him to send more workers into his fields."
MATTHEW 9:37–38 NLT

God has given you a task. Are you ready to go to work? He wants to send you out to meet people who need to know His Son, Jesus. People are ready to be found, and He wants you to tell them. Who knows—maybe this time they'll accept God's "life preserver."

You must realize, however, that this rescue is not all about you—it's about God and His long-term commitment to finding new people to rescue. Jesus said, "The harvest is great," which is good news. But He also said, "The workers are few." Why? Well, all of us love hearing of Christians who tell sinners about Jesus, but few of us want to *do it.*

Today, pray to the God who wants to rescue, and then ask for a place in His story. Then. . .be willing to speak.

» THINK ABOUT IT

- Is anything preventing you from being one of God's harvest workers?

- Why do people matter so much to God?

- How should God's view of people change the way you see them?

» PRAY ABOUT IT

- Think about the way God has changed you.

- Thank Him for making this change.

- Tell God that you're willing to join His harvest crew.

I'm changed because of You, Lord. As a result, I want You to change others too. If You can use me to bring someone to the point of rescue, then I want to be willing.

68. Love Is Not a Consumer

Because of the LORD's great love we are not consumed, for his compassions never fail. They are new every morning; great is your faithfulness.
LAMENTATIONS 3:22–23 NIV

Anger can give birth to hatred, and hatred consumes. It takes what is right and turns it upside down. It promotes holding grudges and being unkind. It occupies the space where good was growing. . .and takes it over.

This *consuming* can change a man, leaving him a shell of his former self. Aren't you glad that God's love isn't a consumer? It replenishes and restores, and it's never used up.

If God were prone to anger, then He'd have the power—and willingness—to destroy anything that stood against Him. But God holds His anger in check and prioritizes love.

Think about how this connects with those who don't follow God. Would anger draw them closer to God or push them away? Lamentations 3 reminds us that because God is faithful, His love keeps us from being consumed. Maybe this is why mercy is a key feature of God's love—God has the right to be consumed by anger, but He chooses love instead.

» THINK ABOUT IT

- Have your choices ever been altered by your anger?

- Why is it impressive that God chooses love instead of hatred?

- How should God's example inspire a change in your choices?

» PRAY ABOUT IT

- Tell God about a time when you responded to someone in hatred.

- Let God know what it means to be loved even after making a wrong choice.

- Ask Him to help you choose His response when others make you angry.

---

*I've been guilty of anger and hatred,
Father. Let Your love change my response
and alter the response of others.*

69. From This Day Forward

*[Jesus said,] "Don't let your hearts be troubled.
Trust in God, and trust also in me. There is
more than enough room in my Father's home.
If this were not so, would I have told you that
I am going to prepare a place for you?"*
JOHN 14:1–2 NLT

There is another reason to pray for the lost. You may not need another reason because you might be sold on the idea of praying for them. However, if you're still indecisive, consider this: some people believe Christianity only helps in this life.

When Jesus died on the cross, His selfless act did two things: (1) forgave sin and (2) offered eternal life. When His rescue plan is accepted, it changes your present *and* future. Jesus is preparing a place for you, and it will be ready when you need it. You probably find comfort in knowing God took an eternal approach in caring for you.

Others can be encouraged by knowing that too. So today, pray that the lost will recognize their need for the rescuer—and make the eternally significant choice to accept Him.

» THINK ABOUT IT

- Why is it important to think about God's entire set of promises when praying for the lost?

- How can you talk with others about an eternal life with God?

- How can prayer make sharing God with the lost more effective?

» PRAY ABOUT IT

- Thank God for taking care of your future.

- Invite Him to change the future for others.

- Ask Him for the opportunity to share His story.

I am grateful, God—today, tomorrow, and forever. The change You've made in me is a change You can make in others. Help me share Your change every chance You give me.

70. The Entrusting

God commendeth his love toward us, in that,
while we were yet sinners, Christ died for us.
ROMANS 5:8 KJV

Commend isn't a word people use much anymore. If you think it sounds a bit like the word *recommend*, then you're pretty close.

To *commend* means to present something as suitable for approval or acceptance. It also means to entrust someone to someone else—which is likely how it's used in Romans 5:8. Paul said that God entrusted us to the love of Jesus. We didn't need to prove we were qualified for redemption—in fact, God entrusted us to the love of Jesus while we still lived in rebellion. There were no exceptions: it was a universally available gift.

Knowing that sinful people were separated from God and would need His love, Christ offered Himself as a sacrifice, showing love to the lost before and after they were found.

Today, entrust a loved one to the love of Christ. Pray for the courage to present Jesus as more than suitable for acceptance. Finally, after you make introductions, ask God to step in and rescue.

» THINK ABOUT IT

- Does the idea of commending someone to Christ remind you of the word *transfer*? How are they connected?

- How have you commended family and friends to Jesus?

- Why is it important to remember that Jesus died for you without expecting your perfection?

» PRAY ABOUT IT

- Admit you're a sinner for whom Christ died.

- Thank Him for the love He gave in spite of your sin status.

- Ask Him to do the same for others.

I was a rebel who needed rescue, Lord. I didn't deserve Your love. Others need to know this same kind of rescue, so reach them with patience and kindness.

71. A Skeptic's Healing

O Lord, if you heal me, I will be truly
healed; if you save me, I will be truly
saved. My praises are for you alone!

JEREMIAH 17:14 NLT

Get reacquainted with the weeping prophet in Jeremiah 17:14. His statement seems like common wisdom, but if that were true, then he probably didn't need to say it.

In Jeremiah's day, many people didn't believe God could heal or save, so they hesitated to offer praise to Him. These people did not believe God was really in control or that He could do the impossible. Jeremiah's words about God's power, therefore, were a revelation to many.

Praying for the skeptical is a way of asking God for their healing. That's what Jesus wanted for Thomas. This disciple doubted what he didn't think was possible, but he too was proven wrong.

While the skeptic pays attention to the outcome, the worshipper gladly proclaims, "God was amazing again today."

Skepticism can be a chronic disease of the heart. We must do more than treat the symptoms; we need healing all the way to the core. Jeremiah knew this, and so does God.

Do you?

» THINK ABOUT IT

- Why could skepticism be considered a disease?

- Why is doubt often a first response?

- How can people find healing from the wounds of skepticism?

» PRAY ABOUT IT

- Admit if you struggle to believe God sometimes.

- Ask for the faith to trust God's unfulfilled promises.

- Thank God for always proving His Word true.

Being a skeptic is easy, Father. Help me do something different. I want to believe what You say and then praise You when You answer prayer.

72. The Perfect Cure

*"He himself bore our sins" in his body
on the cross, so that we might die to
sins and live for righteousness; "by his
wounds you have been healed."*
1 PETER 2:24 NIV

Everyone who's ever lived has been wounded. This includes physical wounds (a cut on the arm), heart wounds (harsh words or a breakup), and soul wounds (a feeling of disappointment with God).

First Peter 2:24 says that when Jesus died on the cross, He created the cure for your hurt. All you have to do is pray for the healing you need. If you had a prescription for a medicine that can cure a fatal disease, would you toss it in the family junk drawer? Of course not! Similarly, God cannot heal you if you refuse to let Him.

This healing has side effects. They may include—but aren't limited to—a death to sin and a life of right living. Thankfully, all these side effects are perfect.

Ask for healing. . .and don't resist the cure. Don't let your spirit, heart, and soul get any weaker. You have a prescription, so fill it in the presence of God's Spirit.

» THINK ABOUT IT

- Why is it wise to understand how God helps the wounded?

- How can the wounding of the heart, soul, or spirit cause long-term issues?

- How can the "prescription" illustration help you understand God's cure?

» PRAY ABOUT IT

- Admit you've been wounded.

- Ask for God's help.

- Accept the cure.

Not every wound heals on its own, God, and I can't heal myself. Would You heal me? Thanks for coming to my rescue one more time.

73. The Healer

He healeth the broken in heart, and
bindeth up their wounds.
PSALM 147:3 KJV

God is like an Emergency Medical Technician (EMT) for the heart. There's no Estimated Time of Arrival (ETA), and there's no need for triage—God knows what you need and how to respond long before you ask. Your call isn't ignored. He knows you need a healed heart that can respond well to His call. If you'll allow Him, He'll treat the wound and let the healing begin.

Your prayers can show how desperately wounded and deeply broken you are. They can include words of pain and sadness, displaying vulnerability that you don't share with anyone else.

You need healing, and God knows it. So *pray* like your life depends on it. *Believe* like you know God can do it. And *wait* like you know help is coming. Don't try nursing your pain on your own or "valiantly" acting as if it doesn't matter.

Some refer to Jesus as the great physician, and King David identified God as the healer. Either way, you have someone on your side who knows wounds will happen. . .and who knows how to treat them when they do.

THINK ABOUT IT

- Why is it normal to act as if your inner pain isn't important?

- What might happen to this pain if you refuse God's help?

- How does it help knowing that God wants to hear from you in the middle of pain?

 PRAY ABOUT IT

- Admit your pain.

- Invite God's help.

- Thank Him for stepping into your overwhelming hurt.

I'm in pain, Lord. Help me now. Before You even show up, I want You to know that I'm grateful for the better days to come.

74. Differently Better

Let all that I am praise the LORD; may I never forget the good things he does for me. He forgives all my sins and heals all my diseases. He redeems me from death and crowns me with love and tender mercies.

PSALM 103:2–4 NLT

God is gracious, and He makes your life differently better than it was before you knew Him.

The phrase *differently better* helps define what it means to be changed by God. If you believe God doesn't really want you to change, then you're left with neither different nor better. You merely think about God from time to time while you trudge along on a road that ultimately leads to nowhere.

He's forgiven you, which means you've made wrong choices. It makes sense to learn what those are and ask for His help in avoiding repeat mistakes. God can also heal all your diseases. This doesn't mean you'll never be sick a day in your life; rather, it means He'll destroy the inner death and decay caused by sin and heal the part of you that will never die. Finally, the psalmist declared that he was redeemed from death, even though his physical body would cease to exist. Why? Because with God, the spirit lives on.

Now *that's* a differently better truth!

» THINK ABOUT IT

- Why does becoming a Christian mean more than just downloading a new app?
- How can past failure and new faith increase the probability of change?
- What might be a good next step in following God?

» PRAY ABOUT IT

- Ask for a healing of the mind.
- Invite God to help you learn His ways.
- Remember His love and mercy.

It isn't natural for me to think like You, Father. Please teach me—I want to learn. Thank You for loving me enough to show mercy when I know I deserve justice.

75. The Intervention

A cheerful heart is good medicine, but
a crushed spirit dries up the bones.
PROVERBS 17:22 NIV

God cares about your body, but He always wants to heal your mind, soul, and spirit. He knows a good attitude changes perspective while anxiety and depression prevent you from freely following His plan.

The great restorer can bring new life to old bones, new thoughts to a broken mind, and new wisdom to a confused spirit. All three require a healing only God can provide. You might start by praying for wisdom, but God cares about your *entire* spiritual condition. You shouldn't push Him away, walk another direction, or place roadblocks between you and Him.

Your physical being can also be healed, but the body was never designed to last forever. It will decay, but what's happening inside can be reviewed daily. Your spirit will outlast your body.

God can use a cheerful heart to counter a crushed spirit, joy to fight against anxious thoughts, and trust to remedy brokenness. God has cures—you just have to access them.

Prayer is the perfect place to start.

» THINK ABOUT IT

- When was the last time you were broken but pretended everything was fine?

- Did that help or hinder you?

- What would a cheerful heart do for your bad days?

» PRAY ABOUT IT

- Admit it when your spirit is crushed.

- Ask God to cheer up your heart.

- Invite God to keep restoring what is missing in your soul.

I need to be healed from a crushed spirit, God. I need cheer in a broken heart. I need Your help to walk freely from a failed past into Your future.

76. Practical Obedience

*My son, attend to my words; incline thine
ear unto my sayings. Let them not depart
from thine eyes; keep them in the midst of
thine heart. For they are life unto those that
find them, and health to all their flesh.*

PROVERBS 4:20–22 KJV

There are many practical reasons for obeying God's rules. And as Proverbs 4:20–22 informs us, better health is one of them. We all know sin can damage our spiritual health, but it might surprise you to hear that it can do the same to us physically.

God said you should not worry, yet if you choose to worry anyway, the stress will produce ulcers, heartburn, stomach aches, and many other issues. Sexual sin also comes with a set of health consequences, and it can further damage the soul, spirit, mind, and heart. Whenever you break one of God's laws, a sharp decline in health is sure to follow.

On the other hand, however, obeying God's rules yields great rewards, and you'll have better health for your body, mind, spirit, soul, and heart.

A medical professional or health-focused website won't give this advice—it comes straight from the mouth of God Himself.

Will you listen?

» THINK ABOUT IT

- Why is health a practical link to obedience?
- How can you improve your health by obeying God today?
- When is the best time to obey God's rules?

» PRAY ABOUT IT

- Honestly consider if you may have health issues related to disobedience.
- Invite God to remind you of His rules.
- Ask Him to help you obey.

I want good health today, Lord. I know You can heal me. I know You want me to obey You. Help me remember Your rules, obey what You ask, and improve my health.

77. Improve Daily Health

Don't be impressed with your own wisdom.
Instead, fear the LORD and turn away
from evil. Then you will have healing for
your body and strength for your bones.
PROVERBS 3:7–8 NLT

Have you ever said something that everyone liked? Maybe they quoted you. Or maybe a local TV station even aired your words on the evening news. That kind of notoriety can leave you feeling impressed with your own ability to discern and articulate truth. It can go to your head and influence your actions.

That can lead to pride, however. Pride leaves God out, even though the words that left your mouth were His idea.

Most would understand your temptation to buy into the press release. Humans want to be validated, to feel like their contribution means something to someone. However, while you can't stop people from saying good things about you, you can make sure people know that anything good flows from your friendship with God. This kind of honesty rescinds any invitation you might have offered to evil, promotes the value of a good God, and improves daily health.

Chase God—not applause. Praise God—not your own efforts. Love God—not the words you speak.

≫ THINK ABOUT IT

- Have you ever made positive comments a priority?
- Why do we tend to long for praise from others?
- How can a priority realignment improve your physical health?

≫ PRAY ABOUT IT

- Confess your innate desire to be affirmed.
- Admit that God is the only one worthy of praise.
- Ask to understand the wisdom of giving God credit.

Sometimes I want to be thought of as important, Father. But I also don't want people to be sidetracked from grasping the importance of knowing You. Become more for me—and for all.

78. The Choice to Heal

At sunset, the people brought to Jesus all who had various kinds of sickness, and laying his hands on each one, he healed them.

LUKE 4:40 NIV

Jesus did what you cannot: He healed. The type of sickness didn't matter to Jesus—He healed anyway. Blindness, disfigurement, weakened limbs, and even death all went down without a fight whenever Jesus spoke.

Sometimes, however, Jesus had the chance to heal. . .but didn't.

If this seems unfair, remember: Jesus isn't a genie, magician, or vending machine. His miracles aren't for sale. If miracles worked this way, there would be no need for hospitals, physicians, health insurance, pharmacies, vitamins, or supplements. Whole industries would go out of business. There will come a day when medical professionals and therapists aren't needed, but for now, they are.

Jesus proved that He can heal, but He also showed that such healing may not be His will sometimes. As hard as it is to understand, God has reasons.

So today, pray for healing—but leave the results to the one who knows best.

» THINK ABOUT IT

- Why do you crave healing when you're in a health crisis?

- How should bad health cause you to trust God even more?

- What does it mean if God doesn't heal you right away? Why?

» PRAY ABOUT IT

- Admit—to yourself and God—when you're physically unwell.

- Confess your trust in God.

- Ask for God's will, even if it doesn't include healing.

Sometimes, health seems more important than You, God. Help me trust Your outcome, even when healing isn't promised.

79. A Strengthened Relationship

*O LORD my God, I cried to you for
help, and you restored my health.*

PSALM 30:2 NLT

Don't hesitate to ask God for better health. He can (and does) perform this kind of miracle for millions each day. Don't believe for a second that God will always say no. Who knows? If you ask Him, He might say yes! So come to God believing wholeheartedly in His power to heal.

God can use medical science, better personal choices, or the words of others. But ultimately, your spiritual healing means more than your physical well-being. Why? Everything God does is designed to strengthen His relationship with you, so when you learn to rely on Him in every situation, this friendship is strengthened.

The very first reading in this book told you that your paths would cross with King David often, and today is no exception. David experienced the miracle of healing, and it seems this miracle took the form of a strengthened relationship between him and the God who gave him the kingdom.

We must remember that physical health is temporary while every other form of healing (mind, heart, soul, and spirit) plays a longer and much more profound role in shaping our identity.

» THINK ABOUT IT

- Why do people respond with more excitement to physical healing than spiritual?

- How can nonphysical healing be the most important?

- What kind of healing is most important to you? Why?

» PRAY ABOUT IT

- Invite God to heal your pain.

- Accept His help, however He offers it.

- Ask for healing, believing He can even if He says no.

My pain isn't more powerful than Your plan, Father. Help me endure while I wait for Your answer.

80. The Overview

*Pleasant words are as an honeycomb, sweet
to the soul, and health to the bones.*
PROVERBS 16:24 KJV

You can say whatever you want. You have the ability to carve deep wounds into someone's soul or to carefully craft sweet words that bring healing to the body.

Over the last few days, you've learned about two sources of healing: God and your choice to obey. Well, you can now add another one to the list: your words. In addition to impacting someone's soul, words can affect the physical body as well. Your words can raise blood pressure, dangerously accelerate the heart, and increase heartburn, or they can lower stress, reduce headaches, and provide a positive atmosphere.

You, therefore, could be part of someone's health plan.

Your choices can impact a person's health in ways that vitamin C gummies and over-the-counter pain killers cannot. So today, pray and ask God to teach you how to improve someone's health with your words.

» THINK ABOUT IT

- How can you improve someone's health by considering what you say to them?

- Why did God make words so important to what happens inside the human body?

- How can this knowledge change what you say and how you say it?

» PRAY ABOUT IT

- Confess whatever hurtful words you've spoken.

- Admit God's words bring healing.

- Ask to learn His way of speaking.

When my words hurt others, Lord, forgive me. Teach me the words that bring healing to those You care about. . .and help me speak them.

81. Declined

*This same God who takes care of me will
supply all your needs from his glorious riches,
which have been given to us in Christ Jesus.*
PHILIPPIANS 4:19 NLT

So many of your everyday needs are things God already takes care of. He's not poor or needy, so if God says no to your requests, it has nothing to do with His ability to supply. Rather, He has some other reason in mind. Maybe it's because what you asked for isn't something you truly need. Or perhaps it might hinder you from following God or even go against His commands. After all, God never gives what His rules forbid.

Keep that in mind the next time you pray. If God's answer is no, then you might want to spend some time learning why. Sometimes, the answer may be hard to discover, but most of the time, all it takes is a little introspection to see that your "need" was more of a "want" all along.

» THINK ABOUT IT

- Why doesn't God agree to give you everything you ask for?

- What might stop a request from getting a positive response?

- How many requests have you made recently that were for actual needs?

» PRAY ABOUT IT

- Invite God to teach you what makes a great request.

- Admit that you might get it wrong.

- Ask for God's help with something you really need.

I want to understand You well enough to make good requests, God. When I fail, teach me. Thank You for taking care of my needs.

82. Obedience Investment

Remember this: Whoever sows sparingly
will also reap sparingly, and whoever sows
generously will also reap generously.
2 Corinthians 9:6 niv

Your actions influence the resources you get to use. Choices, therefore, become more important.

God wants to help people, and you may be the one He chooses to use. If so, you can either look forward to helping or refuse. If you refuse, help will come from another God-inspired source—but why would you want to miss out on honoring God through your obedience? Your generosity will be translated into a personal blessing from God. It may not be a financial return, but it will be a blessing nonetheless.

This is the concept of sowing and reaping. Just as you plant a crop in anticipation of a harvest, you get to see God's crop grow and His harvest collected whenever you're willing to help Him work. Part of the blessing is knowing that God has included you in His plan.

When you have a need, you should understand that God will use others to help you. . .just like He can use you to help them.

» THINK ABOUT IT

- Does the prospect of joining God's adventure seem intimidating?

- Why does the idea of helping others seem both appealing and inconvenient?

- How can you pay attention to what God is doing and then choose to help?

» PRAY ABOUT IT

- Honestly confess your level of interest in helping others.

- Ask God for courage to assist those in need.

- Invite God to answer someone's prayer with your willingness.

Sometimes, I don't feel like helping people, Lord. Yet this is how You often work. Help me be willing to be Your answer to someone's prayer.

83. Celebrating Kindness

I have shewed you all things, how that so labouring ye ought to support the weak, and to remember the words of the Lord Jesus, how he said, It is more blessed to give than to receive.

ACTS 20:35 KJV

When you give a gift to a child at Christmas, what do you pay attention to the most—their enjoyment as they open your gift or the presents bearing your own name? You don't need God's Word to know that sometimes, the gifts you give mean more to you than any gift you might receive in return.

Acts of kindness often mean as much to the one who initiates them as they do to the ones who receive them. The pleasure you have from passing along an act of kindness is something you remember long after the sun sets.

Supporting the weak and needy has nothing to do with superiority—after all, we've all been weak and needy at some point. Rather, such kindness helps the recipient maintain a positive memory in times of struggle.

The idea of Christians caring for others isn't new, and it requires your participation today.

» THINK ABOUT IT

- How can your kindness impact you as much as it impacts whoever received it?

- What benefits come with your act of kindness?

- Why does God say that giving is preferred to getting?

» PRAY ABOUT IT

- Think of people you can show kindness to today.

- Ask God to bless them.

- Invite God to help you remember them.

I want to be kind, Father, and You want that too. Bless those who need kindness and help me to remember to show it.

84. Help Needed Sign

Suppose you see a brother or sister who has no food or clothing, and you say, "Good-bye and have a good day; stay warm and eat well"—but then you don't give that person any food or clothing. What good does that do?

JAMES 2:15–16 NLT

There are two common methods that God uses to take care of your needs: your ability to work and the generosity of others. *But wait,* you may think, *aren't these just human efforts?* Yes and no. While God loves to help, He's also a fan of labor. He doesn't value work just because it helps you earn a living—He values it because it allows you to help others.

God uses His people to help meet needs. So if you say something like, "Well, I'll work just enough for me to eat, stay warm, and pay my bills," then you're missing the compassion that God can pour into your life and cause to overflow into the lives of others.

God could take care of everything without anyone's help, but your help makes a difference in you. It serves to reduce selfishness and allows you to be a positive representative of God's mercy.

» THINK ABOUT IT

- Why is it easy to think people should meet their needs on their own?

- Does selfishness ever interfere with your willingness to help?

- What is your greatest challenge in helping others?

» PRAY ABOUT IT

- Confess that it can be uncomfortable to help others.

- Admit that you should help.

- Ask for the courage to represent God to those who struggle.

Helping others seems intimidating, God, but it's what You ask. Help people see You in my choice to help.

85. Bring the Needs

"Give us each day our daily bread."
LUKE 11:3 NIV

You have needs—personal, professional, and persistent. For most people, prayer for any of these isn't their first choice. Instead, they may rely on their own skill, tenacity, and stubbornness. It might even seem to be working. They feel like they're making up for other people whom they believe rely on God too much.

This choice doesn't save God any time, however—when pride replaces prayer, it leads you further from your relationship with Him. God designed humans to rely on Him and to be reliable in helping others. But if you think He's not worth relying on, you might begin wondering if you really needed rescue at all.

In Jesus' model prayer in Luke, He said, "Give *us*." Why didn't He say, "Give *Me*"? Because Jesus wasn't praying for just His own needs but for the needs of others. He intentionally brought the people's vast needs to the God who knew how to meet them.

When you pray for personal needs, include others who have similar needs. You don't need to stop with yourself.

» THINK ABOUT IT

- How might your prayers' effectiveness be improved when you include others?
- How does pride hinder prayer?
- How can God intervene in selfless prayer?

» PRAY ABOUT IT

- Admit that the needs of others are important.
- Ask God to help everyone who shares the same need as you.
- Invite God to pull pride from the roots of your prayer life.

You want to help everyone, Lord, and You want me to care for the needy. I want to pray for them like I would pray for my own needs, so remove pride from my heart.

86. Created Things

*God created everything.... He made the
things we can see and the things we can't
see.... He existed before anything else,
and he holds all creation together.*
<small>COLOSSIANS 1:16–17 NLT</small>

All the things that qualify as personal needs are made using things God created. Everything you see—and everything you don't even know exists—God holds together like a divine super glue.

Nothing existed before God, and everything that exists now was made with things God made. No one can make anything from elements that He didn't create.

No matter what your greatest personal need is, it began as a gift from God. Humans, however, are masters at using God's creation to make unnecessary things—and then placing them on a pedestal above God.

If you need anything, pray to the God who made it. He made everything so that you can enjoy it, and His creation can bring you satisfaction. You can't exist without using the things made from what God created—only He can ultimately meet your needs.

» THINK ABOUT IT

- How does knowing that God made everything expand your view of how He provides?

- Why is it important to remember that everything falls apart if God doesn't keep it together?

- When you think of God's creation, what are you most grateful for?

» PRAY ABOUT IT

- Spend time before prayer thinking about God's creation.

- Spend time during prayer telling God that you're paying attention.

- Spend time after prayer just being grateful.

The things I love and need are formed by things You made, Father. Your creation is as amazing as Your willingness to provide.

87. The Giving Overflow

Give, and it shall be given unto you;
good measure, pressed down, and
shaken together, and running over.

LUKE 6:38 KJV

In order to have, you cannot keep.

This paradoxical statement makes perfect sense in God's economy. His rules for any return on your investment in the lives of others is different than you may have thought. When you keep what He shares, you somehow end up with less. When you give what God meant for you to share, there somehow seems to be no decrease. This doesn't make sense on paper, and traditional math can't explain it. Perhaps an illustration would help.

When a new child is born into a home, you love that child deeply. When a second child arrives, you don't divide your love in half and grant one part to each; no, you show 100 percent of your love to both. How? Your ability to love expands. Similarly, whenever you give, your blessings overflow and just keep overflowing.

Today, pray that God would help you trust His math and obey His rules on giving. What He's asking may seem impractical —but it's not impossible.

» THINK ABOUT IT

- Do you hesitate when considering the idea of giving to someone?

- Does God's plan for giving seem impossible to you?

- How might you trust God enough to give His plan a try?

» PRAY ABOUT IT

- Admit that giving doesn't always make sense to you.

- Ask God for opportunities to share.

- Thank Him for the love He gives when you share.

I can't explain how I can give yet still have enough, God. May I recognize the opportunities You send and watch You love people through my gift.

88. Involve Yourself in His Plan

"Give as freely as you have received!"
MATTHEW 10:8 NLT

God cares about the things you need. His plan to meet these needs is rational and practical—all you have to do is follow His example. Give with the same freedom with which you've received. . .and don't get gnarled up inside thinking that it isn't fair.

Could you imagine if God decided to do that? What if He wanted to keep all the air, water, and food for Himself, deciding that it's just too much trouble to create more? Even worse, what if He decided that loving you took too much of His time?

Thankfully, God cares for your needs so much that He gives you something every day—His faithfulness isn't part-time. Consequently, you too can give because you know what it's like to receive. God isn't asking for one or two people to step up. He wants *everyone* who receives to share, thus demonstrating His love, meeting the needs of others, and distributing blessings among all people.

This isn't a trick to get you to do His work; rather, it's a chance to be a part of God's plan. Be honored that He wants you involved.

» THINK ABOUT IT

- How is your involvement tied to personal blessing?
- When have you seen God meet your needs through others?
- Do you believe God's plan is practical?

» PRAY ABOUT IT

- Tell God you are willing to be part of His plan.
- Ask Him to show you what to give and where.
- Invite Him to teach you how.

Sometimes it's frightening to say that I'm willing to give, Lord. I don't know what will be required. Show me what, where, and how to give in a way that pleases You and helps others.

89. Outrageously Persuasive

"You alone are the LORD. You made the heavens, even the highest heavens, and all their starry host, the earth and all that is on it, the seas and all that is in them. You give life to everything, and the multitudes of heaven worship you."

NEHEMIAH 9:6 NIV

If God didn't inspire people to help others, there would be no hospitals, churches, or orphanages. People wouldn't adopt children, soup kitchens wouldn't run, and those in prison would have no help.

God made the night sky, and it's yours to enjoy and explore. He made the earth and left you to dig, mow, or move it in whatever way seems best to you. He made the sea, and you can swim, fish, or boat within its waves. Life itself exists because God made and sustains it.

What an elaborate, complex, and outrageously persuasive proof of His goodness!

You should be left with a sense of awe, wonder, and gratitude that transitions beautifully into prayer. Take what you learn about the value of God's gift and choose to pass on His love.

Love is the virtue that gives, cares, and helps. It invites companionship and leads people to worship the God who changed you.

» THINK ABOUT IT

- Why would God choose to give you what you need before you trusted Him?
- How can the things God created cause you to worship Him?
- Why is God's selfless example a good starting place for you?

» PRAY ABOUT IT

- Express a willingness to walk with others.
- Admit you may be out of your comfort zone.
- Ask God for the courage to share anyway.

Walking with others means I have another friend, Father. Even when I feel uncomfortable, help me share You and Your gifts with others.

90. Hoarding, Hiding, and Hindering

[Jesus said,] "I tell you not to worry about everyday life—whether you have enough food and drink, or enough clothes to wear. Isn't life more than food, and your body more than clothing?"

MATTHEW 6:25 NLT

Anxiety disrupts the way God meets needs. You may have a need, but if anxiety prevents you from asking, then the answer is always no. Anxiety makes it impossible to trust that God can take care of things. And even when He gives you an answer, anxiety clouds your ability to recognize it, keeping you fearful of the things God said were not worth worrying over. Anxiety disrupts communication because it makes you panic, which hinders your ability to listen and speak.

Life isn't just about what foods you eat, and your body isn't just a hanger for your wardrobe. When you distill the importance of life down to a small group of essentials, you impair your spiritual vision. You can't see where you're going or how far you've come—you only see what's lacking in the moment.

Worry will continue offering *what if* questions to distract you: "What if I don't have enough?" "What if I don't get any more?" "What if someone takes what I have?"

So stop hoarding and hiding; instead, let God be free to amaze your believing heart.

» THINK ABOUT IT

- How are the prayers of the anxious a statement of disbelief?

- What can you do to combat anxiety through prayer?

- Why does an anxious spirit lack faith?

» PRAY ABOUT IT

- Admit when you're anxious.

- Invite God to make Himself real to you.

- Ask for a brave heart and keep praying.

Lord, whenever I'm worried, I can come to You with a sense of dread. Help me to know You're always with me and focus my thinking enough to pray.

91. Learning Contentment

I have learned to be content whatever the circumstances. I know what it is to be in need, and I know what it is to have plenty. I have learned the secret of being content in any and every situation, whether well fed or hungry, whether living in plenty or in want.

PHILIPPIANS 4:11–12 NIV

A perfect next step in life—and in prayer—is to turn worry into an opportunity to focus on the things God has provided. Anxiety will cause you to focus on things you don't have but are convinced you need; contentment focuses on what you *do* have and realizes it's all you need.

Where Matthew 6:25 describes an obsession with food and clothing, Philippians 4:11–12 describes the opposite—complete trust in God. Paul didn't need a divine meal kit to know God would provide. Paul probably got hungry, but his contentment prioritized God over the things God could give.

Circumstances can't change God's goodness, but your response changes how much you value God and His provisions. Don't be an anxious person who worships the things and not the Creator of things; instead, seek contentment in prayer. Pursue freedom that takes you away from anxiety.

Contentment and anxiety are both responses to stress. Maybe it's time to express the better response.

Stop worrying—discover contentment.

» THINK ABOUT IT

- What makes contentment a more practical choice?
- Why would God prefer contentment over anxiety when hearing from you?
- How will you show contentment with the life God has given you?

» PRAY ABOUT IT

- Admit when contentment seems impossible.
- Welcome God to make the impossible possible.
- Ask for the wisdom to embrace contentment.

Being okay with difficulty doesn't seem possible, Lord. Guide my choices to turn worry into satisfaction with You.

92. Pay Attention to Their Struggle

*I pray that your hearts will be flooded with light
so that you can understand the confident hope
he has given to those he called—his holy people
who are his rich and glorious inheritance.*

Ephesians 1:18 nlt

What if when you told people you were praying for them, you were actually specific about what your prayer included? Your statement would look less like a cliché and more like an honest concern about their struggle. It would prove that you listen and care enough to bring their prayer before the only one who can create a good outcome out of a bad situation.

Do you do this?

The apostle Paul told the people of Ephesus that he regularly prayed for them. But then he went further, telling the contents of his prayers as well. This proved that Paul was paying attention to their struggles.

Loving people means truly listening to them—they know when you aren't, after all. You won't earn your friends' trust if you don't pay attention to the things they struggle with.

Take a lesson from God. He always listens to you. . .and you can know it.

» THINK ABOUT IT

- Are others sometimes underwhelmed by your promise to pray?

- How can telling people the content of your prayers change things?

- How can you put this idea to use today?

» PRAY ABOUT IT

- Learn what your friends are struggling with.

- Invite God into these very specific areas.

- Honestly tell your friends exactly how you're praying for them.

---

*It's not hard to believe that friends struggle,
Father. I know this because I struggle too.
Help me listen to them and give a report to
You. . .and then let them know what I've prayed.*

93. The Destitute

He will regard the prayer of the destitute,
and not despise their prayer.
PSALM 102:17 KJV

Being destitute means lacking the basic necessities of life. It means being poor without a way to change direction. It means being stuck with terrible options—or maybe none at all. It means reaching rock bottom and searching in vain for the light at the end of the tunnel.

The Bible tells us what to do when we find ourselves in this situation—pray. God welcomes the prayers of the despised, desperate, and destitute. He will not ignore their cries. This is great news for any man who thinks he needs to wait for a better day to pray to God. Now is the right time—no waiting. He never delays His response until you seem more presentable. No—He's waiting on you now to speak the word *help*.

Don't act like you need to "save up" to buy a prayer. His assistance is free, and He never rejects the prayers of the humble.

Prayer isn't just for people who have their lives in better shape than yours. Prayer is for you—right here and right now.

» THINK ABOUT IT

- Have you ever decided to wait until you're in better shape to pray?

- Why is this a faulty conclusion?

- How can you take what you know and make a change today?

» PRAY ABOUT IT

- Admit you need help.

- Ask for assistance that only God can give.

- Be wise enough to accept the help He offers.

I can't do life alone, God. I'm not perfect, and I need help. Connect my heart to Your love and remind me that You always make things better.

94. You Get To

*Rejoice in. . .confident hope. Be patient
in trouble, and keep on praying.*
ROMANS 12:12 NLT

Once you're convinced you can pray, you have new opportunities to explore and you have access to joyful hope. You can be patient when trouble comes, knowing God isn't slow in keeping His promises. When you need reassurance, you don't *have* to pray—you *get* to. It's a privilege. . .and an impressive adventure.

Life has never been easy. It will be one day, but not now. That comes at the finish line for those who choose to follow God. Also, this physical life won't last forever. No human being is immortal on earth. That's why it's impossible to have the best life here and now.

The old hymn said it best: Christians are just "passing through" this world. Death isn't the end of the journey, so there's no need to treat it as such. Therefore, out of all the choices you have, stack these three on top: (1) rejoice because you have hope, (2) be patient because trouble is temporary, and (3) pray because God wants to hear from you.

 THINK ABOUT IT

- What are the benefits of a long-range view of life with God?

- How does it help knowing that bad times aren't forever?

- When will you hope, be patient, and pray?

≫ PRAY ABOUT IT

- Confess that you are not always in the mood to rejoice.

- Admit that rejoicing is what God wants.

- Ask God to adjust your perspective.

There are days when rejoicing feels impossible,
Lord. I know it's what You command, so
I ask You to change my perspective.

95. A Wrong Motivation

*When you ask, you do not receive, because
you ask with wrong motives, that you may
spend what you get on your pleasures.*
JAMES 4:3 NIV

If your prayer sounds anything like "God, give me what I want because I want it," then it should come as no surprise when He responds, "Request denied." Because He understands that some of what you ask for stems from a wrong motivation and might get you into trouble, His care prevents Him from saying yes to these demands.

When you get money, do you immediately think about spending it on things you want? If you don't consider how to use that money to help someone else, there's a good chance your prayers are largely about *you*. When you ask God for something, pay attention to His answer. It may indicate that your request falls beneath God's best for you.

You're entitled to God's Word, His love, and His forgiveness —all you must do is believe, apply what you learn, and obey His rules. You're entitled to everything you need, not everything you want.

» THINK ABOUT IT

- How can pride disrupt the motives behind your prayer?

- How is obedience connected to prayer approval?

- Why is it wrong to treat God as if He owes you something?

» PRAY ABOUT IT

- Admit that you might not always get it right when asking God for things.

- Ask God to help eliminate requests that He's already denied.

- Invite His Spirit to teach you the difference.

I will sometimes ask for things You've already said aren't for me, Father. Help me to learn what those are so I can move forward to better prayers.

96. No Waiting

As soon as I pray, you answer me; you encourage me by giving me strength.
PSALM 138:3 NLT

God doesn't have to think about your prayer request as if it were something He'd never considered. He doesn't have to ponder whether or not it's a good fit for you. He doesn't need time as if His mind could be changed. He knows the answer—and He gives the answer immediately, even if you don't recognize His response.

His "wait" might make you think "no," and His "no" might make you think "wait." Even His "yes" can still take time—after all, He may be moving in people's hearts to answer your request. Just as a postcard takes time to reach its destination, the people whom God often uses to convey His answer aren't always as quick as He is. But rest assured: if God has said yes to your request, then it *will* happen.

Don't leave today without considering the last half of Psalm 138:3: "You encourage me by giving me strength." Fix this sentence firmly in your mind and think about what that might look like. How much extra courage do you need in order to share what God's done for you? How much extra strength is yours when you realize just how connected God is to your need?

Find out how much. . .and then share it.

THINK ABOUT IT

- Why is it discouraging when you don't understand God's answer?

- How can you improve your understanding of His answers?

- How can you respond to God's answer with courage?

 PRAY ABOUT IT

- Ask.

- Seek.

- Knock.

I pray because I have a need, God.
I seek because You have answers.
I knock because we need to talk.

97. Prayer Can Fix Broken Things

I waited patiently for the LORD; and he inclined unto me, and heard my cry. He brought me up also out of an horrible pit, out of the miry clay, and set my feet upon a rock, and established my goings. And he hath put a new song in my mouth, even praise unto our God: many shall see it, and fear, and shall trust in the LORD.

PSALM 40:1–3 KJV

God does something amazing with broken things. He looks at what you were and says, "It's not good enough." But He doesn't grab some spiritual twine and glue to hold the old you back together. He does something much better—He takes you out of the mess you're in, sets you in the light of His love, remakes you, gives a new song, and places you before an audience. Even more, He gives you a fresh belief and allows you to talk freely with Him.

When a man who seems destined for a spiritual junkyard finds his way to God, it really is big news. Others notice when the filth that once defined him is removed. They see the change in his conversations and responses. They watch eagerly, wanting to know if God really can make a new creation out of broken lives.

People are watching you today. What do they see?

» THINK ABOUT IT

- How can the contrast between your old and new life become a great conversation starter?

- How does being remade fundamentally alter your story?

- Who gets the credit for the change? Why?

» PRAY ABOUT IT

- Admit you are broken.

- Ask for new life.

- Thank God for making all things new.

Who I'm becoming is not who I once was, Lord. You're doing what I never could: You're changing me. Please don't stop this amazing work.

98. Listen—Talk—
Listen Again

*Dear friends, let us continue to love one another,
for love comes from God. Anyone who loves is
a child of God and knows God. But anyone who
does not love does not know God, for God is love.*

1 JOHN 4:7–8 NLT

When God answers your prayers, you may feel unworthy of His attention. But as gratitude works its way into your heart and mind, you begin recognizing the reason for God's mercy—love.

This love that He spreads over you more thickly than peanut butter on toast isn't meant to stop with you. Instead, you should use that love to nurture friendships, repair relationships, and confuse enemies. God is the embodiment of love, and He wants you to show His example to every curious, seeking, and down-and-out person you encounter. It's impossible to share God's love if you haven't experienced it yourself. Trying to do so will only result in confusion and embarrassment.

To love someone means getting close and stepping into that person's shoes. Love wants to know more. It asks questions and seeks answers. It listens, talks, and listens again.

Are you willing to love like this?

» THINK ABOUT IT

- How is love connected to prayer?

- How can love impact what you pray about?

- Why should love show up in your actions after prayer?

» PRAY ABOUT IT

- Confess that loving other people is not a natural response.

- Admit that you need God's help to love others.

- Invite God's love to remind you how to do the same.

It's easy to love a few people, Father. Loving everyone seems harder, but it's what You ask me to do. Keep showing me how to do what You keep doing for me.

99. More Than Just Words

The Lord says: "These people come near to me with their mouth and honor me with their lips, but their hearts are far from me. Their worship of me is based on merely human rules they have been taught."

ISAIAH 29:13 NIV

When you try to honor God with your words, does it sometimes seem like your prayer has less power than a dead cell phone? If so, ask yourself: Why are you saying these words? Because you mean them? Or because that's what you're supposed to do? If your words lack passion, power, and perspective—if they come not from your deepest struggles but rather from a memorized list—your lips will move but your heart will be someplace else.

Childhood prayers may bring you comfort and nostalgia, perhaps even creating an emotional connection to people you've known. But do they connect you to the God to whom you pray?

If you see the sample prayer at the end of this reading as just another string of words to recite, then ignore it and pray your own prayer. Make it personal. Make it a powerfully real connection to the God who continues to use the Bible to respond to you personally. Learn to infuse relatability into your prayer life. It will be an improvement.

» THINK ABOUT IT

- Why should prayer be personal?
- How can prayer be passionate?
- What are you most concerned about? How can you make it a prayer?

» PRAY ABOUT IT

- Share what's on your mind.
- Pray what's on your heart.
- Ask for what you really need.

Help me gather my thoughts, God. Help me recognize my greatest need. Give me fresh words to share old struggles.

100. The Words God Spoke

All Scripture is inspired by God and is useful to teach us what is true and to make us realize what is wrong in our lives. It corrects us when we are wrong and teaches us to do what is right. God uses it to prepare and equip his people to do every good work.

2 TIMOTHY 3:16–17 NLT

Don't think of this as the end of your journey—think of it as your first step into a new one. Once you grasp the meaning behind a life defined by prayer, you'll need to embrace God's answer. That answer is available in the Bible. Read it, knowing it contains an answer to your prayer, a love that inspired the answer, and a plan to change your future. It can teach, correct, and equip you for every step you'll take.

Let today's reading serve as your commission to take God's good news into the world, and remember that prayer is your connection to God and that His Word is His connection to you.

If you try to go it alone, you're bound for failure. Some days, you'll find yourself standing alone with Jesus because no one else will stand with you; on most days, however, you'll have Christian friends who remind you to step up, walk on, and stand strong.

Walk with God. The journey just keeps getting better.

» THINK ABOUT IT

- Why is the Bible the great supplement to prayer?

- What questions will you try to resolve by reading the Bible?

- How will you use what you've learned to grow your faith?

» PRAY ABOUT IT

- Admit you're still seeking answers to tough questions.

- Invite God to answer through His Word.

- Thank Him for the honor of prayer.

Every day, I have new questions, Lord. And every day, You have answers for me in Your Word. Thanks for this journey in prayer. May I never stop walking toward You.

Another Great Resource for Guys

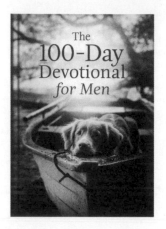

The 100-Day Devotional for Men offers relatable, real-life wisdom and inspiration for everyday living. Men of all ages will encounter page after page of biblical truths they can apply to every area of their lives. With topics like Family, Courage, Culture, Stress, Wisdom, Priorities, Strength, and more, these devotions will encourage readers to grow in their faith and spend regular time in the heavenly Father's presence.

Hardback / 978-1-63609-454-0